Feel Great, Look Great

Balanced Eating for a Balanced Life

Julie Freeman , MA, RD, LD, RYT
Nutritionist

ISBN: 0692331816
ISBN 13: 9780692331811

Introduction

While there are many cookbooks flooding the shelves of bookstores, few combine flavor and simplicity with elegance as an opportunity for portion control. *"Feel Great, Look Great ... Balanced Eating for a Balanced Life",* will be the first in a series of *"Feel Great, Look Great ... from the inside out"* series. This resource provides various substitutes with similar nutrient values. For example Rosemary Pork Tenderloin can be substituted with Chicken Piccata, as well as Oven Roasted Sweet Potatoes with Savory Grains. This creates a unique character for the book. The **Make It A Meal** suggestions offer creative meal options for those with less experience putting meals together that have complementary flavors. Also, for those who prefer paleo or vegan/vegetarian, the options are easily accommodated!

A very timely topic to consider when choosing ingredients for the preparation of these delicious meals is whether or not organic, non-GMO products are important. This is a hot debate at the moment! In my personal and professional research about farming techniques, I do believe that using mostly organic food and certainly non-GMO grown crops is important. At the very least look at the "dirty dozen" list of fruits and vegetables that are most contaminated and whenever possible, choose grass-fed animal products. My second choice would be hormone and anti-biotic free meat and poultry.

My background begins with my personal experience around food, diet and being very overweight. I was a normal weight kid until the age of seven, when my path began toward weight gain, compulsive overeating and sugar addiction. By the time I was nine years old, I was on my first diet along with my parents, who also struggled with being overweight. From then on, the obsession with food and dieting began. I became intrigued with cooking and my mom encouraged my interest by allowing me to help in the kitchen. I became a great baker by adolescence and frequently brought my creations as gifts around holidays and other special occasions to friends, family and the elderly. The "Food Is Love" theme too often in my life, for better and worse.

Speed ahead to college days. My college education was in the Home Economics division of Foods and Nutrition, thus food preparation, the science behind cooking and baking, the ambiance around food, were all as important as learning about diseases and how to treat with special diets. I became intrigued once more with how to create food that was not only delicious to the eyes and palate, but also had more nutritional value. I chose to create a project with my weight control class while working post-grad in the Health Promotion Department of my local hospital. I asked members to bring in two favorite recipes and I spent the entire summer hand-calculating exchanges, limits for fat, sodium and sugar, and produced my first spiral-bound cookbook through an organization that promotes for fund-raisers. This was before the days of computer assisted nutrition analysis. It was such a hit 35 years ago, that I have been asked since that time when I would really publish. Here I am, requesting your time and expertise to assist me in a dream come true for myself and thousands of patients, family and friends who love my creations! Please look at the Introduction for more details about this unique project.

Yours in Health,
Julie Freeman

Acknowledgements

I am grateful to the many folks who have inspired me over the years to make this book a reality:

Lindsay and Ashley, my daughters, who cheer me on and taste the great and not so great experiments;

Stephanie Travers, recent college nutrition graduate, who analyzed each recipe for nutritional adequacy and checked the balance for the Make It A Meal suggestions;

Carmela Cooke, my business assistant, who edited the book to create a uniform structure, flow and ease of readability;

Dot and Bill Fernekees, my parents, who fostered my love for cooking as a child and young adult;

My professors at Framingham State University, Ms. Bangs, Mrs. Baker and Dr. Jordan, who provided me an excellent education not only in the nutritional sciences but also in Home Economics;

Students from my weight control classes in the past who have provided favorite recipes for my analysis and reformulation;

Cooking Light and Diabetic Cooking Magazines, for many recipes that I have further adapted to meet criteria for this cookbook.

Foreword

After years of practicing family medicine with a specialty in allergies and functional gastrointestinal disorders, I know that one of the keys to good health is a healthy diet. On one hand, it is sad to see how many people do not value a healthy diet or have the skills to prepare a meal rich in nutrients. On the other, it is remarkable to see the health benefits and the sense of wonder that people experience when they pay attention to their diet. For some, it is an increased sense of well-being. For many, it is the difference between debilitating illness and health. The hardest parts are convincing people that they need to change their lifestyle--and then showing them how.

It is not easy to find practical information about how to make this lifestyle change happen. ***Feel Great, Look Great – Balanced Eating for a Balanced Life*** offers the opportunity for creating delicious, yet healthy meals, even for those with limited time or skills in the kitchen. Julie Freeman, author of the book, has been counseling individuals and families, has been featured on television and has taught from elementary to the university level for many years. I have known her and worked alongside Julie as a colleague for several years. I have personally witnessed many transformations that her/our patients have enjoyed from adopting her recommendations. Exciting people about nutrition and health is what she is about. Her enthusiasm comes through in this book – a resource for any kitchen.

Feel Great, Look Great – Balanced Eating for a Balanced Life will assist the healthy individual as well as the patient with a medical issue. There are suggestions for food allergies, celiac disease and gluten sensitivity. The menus are calorie-controlled for patients needing weight management assistance. Julie has also made sure that sodium, fat, sugar and fiber are regulated, which will assist in managing cardiovascular,

diabetes and gastrointestinal disorders. The book is written simply and provides assistance with creating an entire meal while maintaining a balanced diet. I look forward to recommending this book to my patients.
Alex Bingham, MD, Director of Allergy, Visions Medical Center

"Feel Great, Look Great . . . Balanced Eating for a Balanced Life"

Julie A Freeman, MA, RD, LD, RYT
Licensed Nutritionist/Registered Yoga Instructor

Marblehead, MA

Juliefreeman57@gmail.com
www.juliefreeman.net

Contents

Appetizers

The appetizers offered in this book provide added interest to any meal or party as well as additional vitamins, minerals and fiber. In addition, the colorful nature of the appetizers will lure anyone to try a new flavor! Legumes are abundant offerings in these appetizers: beans provide protein, soluble fibers, B vitamins. Lettuce wraps are low in calorie and fat and provide some protein in the chicken and curried tomato spread is rich in lycopene, an antioxidant that protects cells from cancer, heart disease and macular degeneration.

Asian Lettuce Wraps

with Hoisin Dipping Sauce

Serves 8

Sauce:
2 tablespoons hoisin sauce
2 tablespoons pomegranate juice
½ teaspoon sugar
½ teaspoon orange rind, grated

Filling:
1 cup cole slaw mix, shredded
2 tablespoons peanuts, toasted
½ jalapeno pepper, seeded, sliced into thin strips
1 teaspoon cilantro, dried
½ cup edamame, shelled, thawed
¼ cup carrots, matchstick
8 inner-leafs green leaf lettuce

Directions:

1. Combine sauce ingredients in small bowl; set aside.
2. In medium bowl, combine filling ingredients except lettuce; toss gently.
3. Arrange lettuce leaves on large serving platter and spoon ¼ of the mixture on each leaf.
4. Drizzle 1 tablespoon of sauce on top; serve.

Nutrient Analysis: cal 43/pro 1.5/carb 6/fiber 1/fat 1.5/sodium 97

Exchanges: 1/2 bread

Make it a Meal: Add 2 cups of diced chicken and pita crisps to create a meal salad.

Adapted from Diabetic Cooking

Curried Tomato Spread

Serves 10

½ cup water
2 cloves garlic, chopped
½ cup fire roasted tomatoes, crushed
½ teaspoon ground cumin
¼ teaspoon curry powder
⅛ teaspoon ground turmeric
⅛ teaspoon crushed red pepper
1 - 16 ounce can cannellini beans, rinsed, drained

Directions:

1. Place water and garlic in a small saucepan; bring to boil. Cook about 3 minutes or until reduced to 2 tablespoons.
2. Add tomatoes, ground cumin, curry powder, turmeric, and red pepper; cook 2 minutes over medium-low heat.
3. Stir in beans and cook 2 minutes more.
4. Place bean mixture into a food processor and process until smooth.

Nutrient Analysis: cal 44/pro 2/carb 8/fiber 2/fat 0/sodium 140

Exchanges: ½ bread

Make it a Meal: Spread on top of salt-free tortilla chips or crackers.

Adapted from Cooking Light Magazine

Rosemary-Chickpea Dip

Serves 12

2 teaspoons olive oil

1 cup green onion, chopped

2 – 15½ ounce cans garbanzo beans (chickpeas), low-sodium, rinsed, drained

1½ teaspoons fresh rosemary, chopped

2 tablespoons lemon juice

¼ cup vegetable broth, non-fat

Directions:

1. Heat oil in large, non-stick skillet over medium-high heat. Add onions; sauté 3 minutes or until tender. Add beans; sauté 1 minute.
2. Place bean mixture along with remaining ingredients in a food processor; process until smooth.
3. Transfer to bowl and serve with items for dipping.

Nutrient Analysis: cal 56/pro 4/carb 12/fiber 4/fat 2/sodium 134

Exchanges: ½ meat, ½ bread

Make it a Meal: Dip with pita wedges or spread over pita bread with sliced cucumbers and tomatoes. Or make into soup by adding vegetable broth.

Adapted from Cooking Light Magazine

Cannellini Pesto

Serves 24

2 - 16 ounce cans cannellini beans, rinsed, drained
1 cup fresh basil leaves
2 tablespoons parmesan cheese, grated
2 tablespoons water
1 teaspoon olive oil
1 clove garlic, crushed
1 tablespoon pine nuts, toasted

Directions:

1. Place all ingredients except nuts in food processor; process until smooth.
2. Add nuts; pulse 5 times or until nuts are chopped.
3. Place in serving bowl.

Nutrient Analysis: cal 38/pro 3/carb 6/fiber 2/fat 1/sodium 105

Exchanges: ½ meat

Make it a Meal: Dip with fresh green beans or celery sticks.

Adapted from Cooking Light Magazine

Red Lentil and Sweet Potato Hummus

Serves 50

1 tablespoon olive oil
1 medium onion, chopped
2 cloves garlic, chopped
1 medium sweet potato, peeled, cut
1 teaspoon ground cumin
1 teaspoon paprika
3½ cups water
22 ounces (about 3½ cups) red lentils, pre-soaked
¼ cup broth, chicken or vegetable, low-salt
¼ cup fresh lemon juice
¼ teaspoon ground black pepper

Directions:

1. In a large saucepan over medium-high heat, warm oil. Add onion and sauté, stirring occasionally, until onion softens, 5-7 minutes.
2. Add garlic, sweet potato, cumin and paprika and sauté 1 to 2 minutes, until spices are fragrant.
3. Stir in water and lentils and bring to a boil. Reduce heat to medium-low, cover and simmer until lentils and sweet potatoes are soft, 15–18 minutes. Let cool.
4. In a food processor or blender, purée lentil mixture with broth, lemon juice and pepper. Taste and adjust seasoning; place in serving bowl.
5. Optional: Drizzle with olive oil and sprinkle with chopped cilantro.

Nutrient Analysis: cal 50/pro 3.5/carb 8.5/fiber 2/fat .5/sodium 3.5

Exchanges: 1/2 meat, 1/2 bread

Serving Suggestion: Spread on top of crackers or pita chips.

Spicy Peanut Dip with Crudités

Serves 40

2 medium sweet red peppers
1 sweet yellow pepper
1 pound baby carrots
1 cup creamy peanut butter, reduced-fat
2 tablespoons soy sauce, low-sodium
1½ tablespoons sake rice wine or rice vinegar
2 tablespoons Worcestershire sauce
2 tablespoons sugar
2 teaspoons sesame oil
2 tablespoons garlic, minced
1 tablespoon ground ginger
7 tablespoons water

Directions:

1. Using a paring knife, cut off the top and bottom of the peppers. Remove seeds and cut each pepper in half lengthwise. Then cut each half lengthwise into 3 or 4 strips, removing any white membrane. Cut each strip into pieces about 1½ inches long.
2. Arrange the peppers and carrots in separate piles in a decorative basket, leaving a small space in the middle for the dip.
3. Put the peanut butter in a blender or a food processor fitted with a steel blade, then add soy sauce, rice wine, Worcestershire sauce, sugar, sesame oil, minced garlic, and ginger, blending until smooth after each addition.
4. Add the water and continue blending. The dip should be stiff but still creamy. If the dip seems too thick, add a little more water; if it seems too thin, add more peanut butter.
5. Scoop into a small bowl and place in the basket of vegetables. Serve.

Nutrient Analysis: cal 52/pro 2/carb 5.5/fiber 1/fat 2.5/sodium 87

Exchanges: 1 vegetable, 1/2 fat

Adapted from Nina Simonds, Whole Foods Market InSeason (2007)

Caramelized Black Bean "Butter"

Serves 10

Cooking spray
1 cup onion, chopped
1 - 15 ounce can black beans, lower sodium, drained, rinsed
1 teaspoon balsamic vinegar
1 teaspoon cocoa, unsweetened
¼ teaspoon paprika
1 teaspoon fresh parsley, chopped

Directions:

1. Heat a large, non-stick skillet over medium-high heat; coat with cooking spray. Add onion; sauté 10 minutes or until golden.
2. Place onion, beans, vinegar, cocoa and paprika in a food processor; process until smooth.
3. Transfer to serving bowl and sprinkle with parsley.

Nutrient Analysis: cal 38/pro 2/carb 10/fiber 2/fat 0/sodium 102

Exchanges: ½ bread

Serving Suggestion: Dip with baked tortilla chips or spread on sandwich of sliced Ciabatta with grilled vegetables and arugula.

Adapted from Cooking Light Magazine

Red Pepper Bean Spread

Serves 12

2 red bell peppers
1 - 15 ounce can kidney beans, lower sodium, rinsed, drained
2 tablespoons tomato paste
½ teaspoon lemon peel, grated
¼ teaspoon ground black pepper
⅛ teaspoon ground red pepper

Directions:

1. Preheat broiler.
2. Cut bell peppers in half lengthwise; discard seeds and membranes. Place pepper halves, skin side up on a foil-lined baking sheet.
3. Broil 10 minutes or until blackened. Place in a zip-top plastic bag; seal. Let stand 5 minutes. Peel and chop.
4. Place bell peppers and remaining ingredients in a food processor and process until smooth.

Nutrient Analysis: cal 40/pro 2/carb 8/fiber 2/fat 0/sodium 62

Exchanges: ½ bread

Serving Suggestion: Toasted bagel chips or raw vegetables or place on top of crostini with a slice of fresh mozzarella.

Adapted from Cooking Light Magazine

Tex-Mex Pinto Bean Spread

Serves 10

1 - 15 ounce can pinto beans, rinsed, drained
½ cup onion, chopped
2 tablespoons fresh cilantro, chopped
2 teaspoons lime juice
½ jalapeno pepper, seeded, chopped
½ cup plum tomatoes, chopped
1 tablespoon pumpkin seeds, toasted

Directions:

1. Place all ingredients except tomato and pumpkin seeds in food processor and process until smooth.
2. Place bean mixture in a bowl; stir in chopped tomato and sprinkle with pumpkin seeds.

Nutrient Analysis: cal 46/pro 2/carb 8/fiber 2/fat 0/sodium 128

Exchanges: ½ bread

Make it a meal: Serve with baked tortilla chips or spread on quesadillas or tacos.

Adapted from Cooking Light Magazine

Soups

Soups are warm, filling or can be part of a light meal with a salad and hearty crisp bread! Soup can be an appetizer before a meal or can provide some fullness for those wishing to limit calories in heavier entrees. Options range from creamy versions that are low in fat to protein rich bean varieties or a melange of phytochemical packed vegetable soups. The choice is yours!

Guidelines for Stock

A well-made stock is at the heart of a good, full-flavored soup. Good stock can easily be made from a variety of kitchen leftovers. Stock can also be used as a flavor-rich basis for casseroles or sauces, and as a flavor enhancer for rice and pasta.

Stocks are made by simmering ingredients for several hours, either on the stove top or in a crock pot. Stocks do take time to prepare, but actually require little work. Simply save leftover bones, pieces of poultry or meat, vegetable trimmings, juices from cooked vegetables, etc. in your refrigerator or freezer (tightly covered) until you have a reasonable quantity. Add these with water and seasonings of your choice to a heavy pot. Simmer, don't boil, and strain off cooked ingredients before storing.

Easy Vegetable Stock

1. Save vegetable trimmings in plastic bag or jar until you have a quart or more (celery, carrots, greens, beans, peapods, potato and squash). Avoid broccoli, cabbage, cauliflower and brussels sprouts. These vegetables tend to have a strong flavor.
2. Put them in a large heavy saucepan, cover with water, and season with a little salt.
3. Cover the pan and bring to a boil, then reduce heat and simmer for an additional 20 minutes or so until the vegetables are cooked but not overcooked.
4. Strain immediately. Cool and refrigerate.

- Bouillon or commercial broths can also be used as stocks. Since these items are very high in sodium, we suggest you look for low sodium varieties or use half the bouillon/broth called for in a soup recipe (make up the rest of the volume with plain water).
- Stocks that contain meat or poultry should be degreased before using. You can skim fat off hot stock by using a slotted spoon or paper towel. You can also add ice to stock and then remove the fat that will congeal as the stock cools.

- We recommend preparing stock at least one day before you plan to use it. Stock can then be refrigerated and fat layer can easily be skimmed off.
- Stock refrigerated in plastic containers will last approximately 1 week.
- Stock frozen in containers or as ice cubes will last up to 3 months.
- Refrigerated or frozen stock should be reheated to boiling after thawing.

Adapted from Massachusetts General Hospital, Boston, MA

Autumn Bisque

Serves 14

½ cup leeks, chopped
½ cup onion, chopped
½ cup celery, finely chopped
2 medium apples, peeled, cored, finely chopped
7 cups chicken stock, lower sodium
4 cups butternut squash, peeled, diced
2 tablespoons butter, whipped, no added salt
2 tablespoons flour
12 ounces boneless chicken breast, roasted, meat only
1 teaspoon dried thyme
½ teaspoon dried sage
¼ teaspoon dried rosemary
½ teaspoon ground turmeric
1 pinch ground nutmeg
1 pinch ground black pepper
½ cup cider
½ cup evaporated skim milk (or use coconut milk)

Directions:

1. In kettle lightly coated with cooking spray, cook leeks, onion, celery and apples. Cook over moderate heat until soft.
2. Add 7 cups chicken stock and simmer for 10 minutes.
3. Add butternut squash and cook the mixture, adding more water if necessary to keep vegetables covered; cook 15 minutes or until tender.
4. In a small saucepan, melt 2 tablespoons butter or dairy-free substitute. Stir in 2 tablespoons flour and cook the roux over low heat, stirring for 3 minutes.
5. Whisk ½ cup soup into the roux and add this mixture into the soup.
6. Add chicken and spices.
7. Simmer soup for 8 minutes, stirring occasionally.

8. Add cider and evaporated skim milk and simmer until heated through.
9. Garnish with chopped parsley and croutons; serve.

Nutrient Analysis: cal 98/pro 9.2/carb 11/fiber 1.4/ fat 2/ sodium 166

Exchanges: 2 Meat, 1 Bread, 1 Fat

Make it a meal: Add 1 serving of *Salad Greens with Honey Mustard Dressing,* 2 ounces turkey and 1 serving of *Crispy Spiced Almond Wontons.*

Minestrone Soup

Serves 16

Cooking spray
½ cup carrot, sliced
½ cup celery, sliced
1 medium onion, finely chopped
5 ounces cut green beans, frozen
2 cups lima beans, canned or frozen
28 ounce can tomatoes, no added salt
2 cups water
¼ teaspoon ground black pepper
¾ teaspoon basil
¼ teaspoon oregano
¼ teaspoon thyme
2 cups kidney beans, boiled, no added salt
1 cup cannellini beans
1 cup parmesan cheese, grated

Directions:

1. Heat skillet and coat with cooking spray.
2. Sauté carrots, celery, and onion for about 3 minutes.
3. Steam green beans and lima beans in steamer for 2 minutes.
4. Combine all ingredients in a pot and simmer until vegetables are tender.
5. Top each serving with 1 tablespoon grated Parmesan cheese.

Nutrient Analysis: cal 115/pro 7.5/carb 17/fiber 4/fat 2/sodium 234

Exchanges: 1 Meat, 1/2 Bread, 1 Veg

Make it a Meal: Serve with a *Simple Side Salad*, 1 ounce diced cooked chicken or turkey, 1/2 ounce fat-free mozzarella cheese, and 1 serving of *Pita Crisps*.

Winter Vegetable Soup

Serves 16

½ pound leeks
1 cup onions, chopped
1 tablespoon olive oil
½ pound carrots, peeled, sliced
½ pound parsnips, peeled, chopped
½ cup dried lentils
½ cup dried split peas
½ cup dried white beans
5 small sprigs fresh thyme (¼ teaspoon dried)
½ teaspoon ground black pepper
8 cups chicken broth, non-fat, low-sodium
1 pound tomatoes, peeled, seeded, chopped (or 1 pound canned Italian plum)
5 ounces fresh spinach, rinsed
½ cup fresh parsley, loosely packed

Directions:

1. Trim leeks, leaving 1 inch of green. Cut leeks in half lengthwise and rinse well. Slice thin.
2. In a large soup pot, sauté leeks and onion in oil over medium heat for 5 minutes or until onions are soft but not browned.
3. Add carrots, parsnips, lentils, peas, beans, thyme, ground pepper, and chicken stock. Bring to boil; reduce heat to simmer, cover, and cook for 45 minutes, stirring occasionally.
4. Add tomatoes and continue to simmer for 15 minutes, until white beans are tender.
5. Add spinach and cook until it is wilted, about 3 minutes.
6. Ladle into soup plates, discarding thyme springs. Scatter with parsley leaves and serve.

Nutrient Analysis: cal 106/pro 6.3/carb 18/fiber 6.3/fat 1/sodium 54

Exchanges: 1 meat, 1/2 bread, 1 vegetable

Make it a Meal: Serve with simple salad with 2 ounces grilled chicken and half-piece of Millet & Flax Lavash (gluten-free).

Baked Vegetable Chowder

Serves 14

1½ cups tomatoes, diced
1 cup green bell pepper, chopped
3 cups zucchini, sliced
2½ cups chickpeas, boiled, no added salt (garbanzo)
4 cloves garlic, minced
1 leaf bay leaves
2 teaspoons dried basil
½ teaspoon paprika
¼ teaspoon ground black pepper
1 cup white table wine
½ cup vegetable broth, low-sodium
¾ cup mozzarella cheese, part-skim, grated
1½ cups skim milk

Directions:

1. Preheat oven to 350°F.
2. Place all vegetables, beans, and seasonings in a large covered casserole.
3. Pour white wine and vegetable broth over mixture and bake covered for 1 hour.
4. Add cheese and milk, stirring just enough to blend. Return to oven and bake covered for an additional 10 minutes, or until mixture is thoroughly heated.

Nutrient Analysis: cal 102/pro 5.7/carb 13/fiber 2.8/fat 2.2/sodium 143

Exchanges: 1 Meat, 1/2 Bread, 1 veg

Make it a Meal: Add 1 slice of turkey bacon, 1/4 cup drained and toasted chickpeas for salad, 1 serving *Carrot Salad* & 1/2 serving *Grilled Garlic Naan.*

Hearty Lentil Soup

Serves 4

¾ cup lentils
2 cups water
½ cup onion, chopped
½ cup celery, minced
½ cup carrot, chopped
1 teaspoon garlic, minced
1 teaspoon olive oil
1 teaspoon dried basil
¼ teaspoon dried oregano
¼ teaspoon ground black pepper
1½ teaspoons molasses
1 teaspoon wine vinegar
½ cup mozzarella cheese, part-skim, shredded

Directions:

1. Simmer lentils in water, covered for 1 hour.
2. Sauté onions, celery, carrot and garlic in olive oil. Add to lentils. Continue to simmer for 30 minutes.
3. Add remaining ingredients to soup 30 minutes before serving. Serve with fresh scallions on top.

Nutrient Analysis: cal 206/pro 13/carb 28/fiber 12/fat 4/sodium 107

Exchanges: 2 Meat, 1 Bread, 1 Fat

Make it a Meal: Add 1 serving *Asian Slaw* and ½ serving *Grilled Garlic Naan*

Split Pea Soup

Serves 6

1½ tablespoons canola oil
½ cup carrots, chopped
¼ cup onions, chopped
1 clove garlic, minced
4½ cups water
¾ cup dry split peas
1 bay leaf
2 teaspoons dry white wine,
½ teaspoon white vinegar
¼ teaspoon crushed thyme
⅛ teaspoon ground black pepper
1 package chicken bouillon, low-sodium

Directions:

1. In large saucepan over medium-high heat sauté carrot, onion, and garlic in oil. Cook about 4 minutes until soft, stirring frequently.
2. Add remaining ingredients, bring to a boil. Reduce heat; cover.
3. Simmer about 1 to 1¼ hours, stirring occasionally.
4. If soup becomes too thick, add additional water. Remove bay leaf before serving.

Nutrient Analysis: cal 105/pro 6/carb 17/fiber 7/fat 1/sodium 118

Exchanges: 1 meat, ½ bread, 1 vegetable

Make it a Meal: Add 1 slice turkey bacon & 1 serving *Mediterranean Orzo Salad with Feta Vinaigrette.*

Cream of Cauliflower Soup

Serves 8

Cooking spray
1 large onion, chopped
3½ cups chicken broth, non-fat, lower sodium
2 carrots, ¼" slices
1 medium head cauliflower, cut into small flowerets
1 cup skim milk
¼ teaspoon ground nutmeg
¼ teaspoon ground black pepper
1 tablespoon dry sherry, (optional)
2 tablespoons fresh parsley, chopped
3 tablespoons protein powder

*Dairy Free option: replace with coconut milk

Directions:

1. In a 4-quart saucepan lightly coated with cooking spray, sauté chopped onion over medium heat. Cook until onion is translucent, approximately 5 minutes.
2. Pour in chicken broth and bring to a boil.
3. Add vegetables to boiling broth and reduce heat. Cover and simmer until vegetables are tender when pierced, about 7 minutes.
4. Pour a small amount at a time into a blender and whirl until smooth. Add protein powder.
5. Return all the puree to pan; add milk, nutmeg, pepper, and sherry. Heat to simmering.
6. Serve garnished with chopped parsley.

Nutrient Analysis: cal 77/pro 8/carb 9/fiber 3/fat 1/sodium 131

Exchanges: 1 Meat, 1/2 Bread

Make it a Meal: Add 1 serving *Salad Greens with Honey Mustard Dressing*, 2 ounces baked ham, 1 serving *Pita Crisps* and 1 serving *Red Lentil and Sweet Potato Hummus*.

Hearty Vegetable Soup

Serves 16

1 teaspoon olive oil
½ cup onion, chopped
½ cup green bell pepper, chopped
½ cup celery, sliced
1 cup (1 medium squash) summer squash or zucchini, sliced
8 ounces boneless, skinless chicken breast, diced
16 ounce can tomatoes, no added salt, cut-up
15.5 ounce can kidney beans, low-sodium
15 ounce can great northern beans
½ cup water
2 teaspoons chili powder
1½ teaspoons dried basil
¼ teaspoon ground black pepper
2 cloves garlic, minced
1 leaf bay leaves
¼ cup cashews or peanuts, no added salt

Directions:

1. In a 4-quart Dutch oven heat olive oil and sauté onion, green pepper, celery, and summer squash/zucchini.
2. Add rest of ingredients except nuts and bring to a boil. Reduce heat, cover, and simmer for 1 hour.
3. Stir in nuts; heat through. Remove bay leaf before serving.

Nutrient Analysis: cal 109/pro 8.5/carb 14/fiber 3.5/fat 2/sodium 72

Exchanges: 1 Meat, 1/2 Bread, 1 Veg

Make it a Meal: Add 1 serving *Waldorf Salad*, 2 ounces roasted chicken & ½ serving *Crispy Spiced Almond Wontons*

Vietnamese Beef and Noodle Soup

Serves 8

4 cups water
1 ounce whole wheat angel hair pasta
2¼ cups beef stock, non-fat, no added salt
1 shallot, sliced
½ teaspoon fresh ginger, minced
1 teaspoon Five Spice Powder
½ teaspoon hot sauce
2 teaspoon soy sauce, low-sodium, wheat-free
12 ounces beef sirloin, boneless, sliced 1/8" thick
⅛ teaspoon ground black pepper
1 cup bean sprouts
2 small green onions, thinly sliced
1 red chili pepper, thinly sliced
2 lime wedges
2 tablespoons fresh cilantro

Directions:

1. Bring water to a boil in a medium saucepan. Cook pasta until tender, about 3 to 4 minutes. Drain; set pasta aside in strainer.
2. Meanwhile, in another medium saucepan bring stock, shallot, and ginger to a boil. Reduce heat and simmer 10 minutes.
3. Stir in five spice powder, hot sauce, and soy sauce.
4. Season sirloin with pepper. Add sirloin and bean sprouts to stock. Cook until beef is no longer pink, about 1 to 2 minutes.
5. Add cooked pasta to soup and stir in green onions.
6. Ladle into bowls; garnish with chili slices, lime juice and cilantro.

Nutrient Analysis: cal 98/pro 12/carb 9/fiber 1/fat 1.5/sodium 105

Exchanges: 2 Meat, 1/2 Bread, ½ vegetable

Make it a meal: Add 1 serving *Asi≠sin Dipping Sauce,* 1 ounce shredded chicken and 1 serving of *Crispy Spiced Almond Wontons.*

Salads

Salads have quickly become a favorite meal or vegetable option in many households. And variety is limitless! From a simple salad to many slaw varieties, the flavors are varied from sweet to more tart. For heartier appetites, there are some grain salads as well. Cold vegetable salads provide many vitamins and minerals in their natural state, preserved from being destroyed by heat.

Asian Slaw

Serves 4

6 cups bagged broccoli slaw
Or
1 cup broccoli, chopped
1 cup green or Savoy cabbage, shredded
2 cups carrot, shredded
2 cups red cabbage, shredded

Dressing:
½ cup plain Greek yogurt, fat-free
1 teaspoon mayonnaise, reduced-fat
1 teaspoon prepared Dijon mustard
2 tablespoons milk, 1% (or rice milk)
1 teaspoon rice vinegarv
1 teaspoon soy sauce, low-sodium
1 teaspoon ginger, minced
1 teaspoon garlic, minced
1 packet Stevia
¼ teaspoon ground black pepper

1 tablespoon raisins

Directions:

1. Put the yogurt in a mixing bowl and add the dressing ingredients, whisking lightly after each addition. Taste and adjust seasoning if necessary.
2. Add raisins to shredded vegetables, pour in the dressing, and toss lightly to coat.
3. Cover with plastic wrap and refrigerate for 1 hour.

Nutrient Analysis: cal 106/pro 6/carb 17/fiber 4/fat 2/sodium 172

Exchanges: 2 vegetable, ½ fat

Adapted from Nina Simonds, Whole Foods Market InSeason (2007)

Mediterranean Orzo Salad

with Feta Vinaigrette

Serves 4

½ cup (about 4 oz.) orzo, uncooked
4 cups baby spinach, pre-washed, chopped
⅓ cup sun dried tomatoes, packed in oil - drained
3 tablespoons red onion, chopped
2 pitted Kalamata olives, chopped
½ teaspoon ground black pepper
½ cup marinated artichoke hearts, w/liquid
½ cup (about 2 oz.)Feta cheese, reduced-fat - crumbled

Directions:

1. Cook orzo according to package directions, omitting salt and fat. Drain and rinse with cold water.
2. In a large bowl, combine orzo, spinach, tomatoes, onion, olives, and pepper.
3. Drain artichokes, reserving the marinade. Coarsely chop artichokes.
4. Add artichokes, reserved marinade and 1/4 cup feta cheese to orzo mixture, tossing gently to coat.
5. Sprinkle each serving with remaining feta.

Nutrient Analysis: cal 176/pro 8/carb 28/fiber 4/fat 4/sodium 385

Exchanges: 1 bread, 2 veg, 1 meat, 1 fat

Make it a Meal: Add 3 ounces of chicken/shrimp or pair with 1 serving of *Split Pea Soup.*

Adapted from Cooking Light Magazine

Salad Greens with Honey-Mustard Dressing

Serves 4

Dressing:
1 tablespoon honey
3 tablespoons Dijon mustard
1 tablespoon olive oil
1 tablespoon shallot, minced
3 tablespoons apple cider vinegar
Salad:
8 cups mixed greens such as; arugula, romaine, radicchio, etc.
½ cup onion, sliced
½ ounce goat cheese, crumbled

Directions:

1. For the dressing, combine all ingredients until well blended.
2. Toss dressing with greens, onion slices, and goat cheese (you will not need all the dressing).

Nutrient Analysis: cal 96/pro 2/carb 11/fiber 1/fat 5/sodium 295

Exchanges: 2 vegetable, 1 fat

Adapted from Cuisine At Home Magazine

Carrot Salad

Serves 2

1 carrot, grated
1 tablespoon raisins
¼ cup pineapple, crushed in juice, drained
1 teaspoon mayonnaise, lowfat
2 teaspoons plain Greek yogurt, fat-free
1 tablespoon walnuts, chopped

Directions:

1. Mix all ingredients. Chill before serving.

Nutrient Analysis: cal 78/pro 2/carb 12/fiber 2/fat 3/sodium 32

Exchanges: 1 vegetable, ½ fruit, ½ fat

Pineapple Cole Slaw

Serves 4

½ head cabbage
2 tablespoons mayonnaise, diet, low-salt
1 tablespoon plain Greek yogurt, fat-free
1 carrot, shredded
8 ounce can pineapple, crushed in juice, drained

Directions:

Mix all ingredients together. Chill before serving.

Nutrient Analysis: cal 87/pro 3/carb 18/fiber 4/fat 2/sodium

Exchanges: 2 vegetable, ½ fruit

Adapted from Jackie Harwood

Simple Side Salad

Serves 2

Salad:
1 cup romaine lettuce, shredded
1 cup spinach leaves
½ cup arugula
½ cup radicchio
½ cup carrot, grated
½ cup cucumber w/peel, sliced
10 cherry tomatoes
½ cup celery, chopped
¼ cup onion, chopped
Dressing:
2 teaspoons olive oil
2 tablespoons white wine vinegar
2 teaspoons fresh basil

Directions:

1. Combine first 9 ingredients in a medium bowl.
2. Whisk together the olive oil, vinegar and basil and toss with salad greens.

Nutrient Analysis: cal 97/pro 3/carb 12/fiber 4/fat 5/sodium 77

Exchanges: 1 vegetable, 1 fat

Cole Slaw

Serves 4 (Approx. 1 cup/serving)

4 cups Cole slaw mix, shredded
¼ cup plain yogurt or almond milk
1 tablespoon mayonnaise, reduced-fat
1 teaspoon sugar or Stevia
1 tablespoon apple cider vinegar

Directions:

Mix all ingredients and let set for two hours or more.

Nutrient Analysis: cal 39/pro 1/carb 6/fiber 1/fat 1/sodium 59

Exchanges: 1 vegetable

Quinoa & Mango Salad

Serves 8

2 cups water
1 cup quinoa, uncooked
2 cups mango, peeled, cubed (about 2 large mangos)
½ cup green onion, sliced
½ cup dried cranberries
2 tablespoons fresh parsley, chopped
¼ cup olive oil
1 tablespoon & 1½ teaspoons white wine vinegar
1 teaspoon prepared Dijon mustard
½ teaspoon sea salt
⅛ teaspoon ground black pepper

Directions:

1. Combine water and quinoa in medium saucepan. Bring to boil.
2. Reduce heat; simmer, covered 10 to 20 minutes until all water is absorbed.
3. Stir; let stand, covered 15 minutes.
4. Transfer to large bowl; cover and refrigerate at least 1 hour.
5. Add mango, green onions, cranberries, and parsley to quinoa; mix well.
6. In a small bowl, combine oil, vinegar, mustard, salt, and pepper. Whisk until blended.
7. Pour over quinoa mixture; mix until well blended. Allow to sit at room temperature for at least 30 minutes before serving.

Nutrient Analysis: cal 191/pro 3/carb 27/fiber 3/fat 8/sodium 171

Exchanges: ½ bread, 1 fruit, 1 ½ fat

Credit: Adapted from Diabetic Cooking

Waldorf Salad

Serves 2

1 apple, chopped
1 stalk celery, chopped
1 teaspoon mayonnaise, diet, low-salt
1 tablespoon plain Greek yogurt, fat-free
½ teaspoon honey
1 tablespoon walnuts, chopped

Directions:

1)   Mix all ingredients. Chill before serving.

Nutrient Analysis: cal 74/pro 2/carb 12/fiber 2/fat 3/sodium 8

Exchanges: 1 fruit, ½ fat

Jicama Salad

Serves 2

1 cup Romaine lettuce, shredded
½ cup cucumber w/peel, sliced
1 cup jicama, sliced
¼ cup fresh coriander (cilantro/Chinese parsley)
2 teaspoons fresh lime juice
2 teaspoons canola oil

Directions:

Mix all ingredients and let set for two hours or more.

Nutrient Analysis: cal 73/pro 1/carb 8/fiber 4/fat 5/sodium 6

Exchanges: 2 vegetable, 1 fat

Sauces

Sauces offer an opportunity to enhance the flavor of many foods. However, most sauces are often high in fat, sugar and calories. There are a variety of ways to use these creations and reformulations without excess fat, sugar and calories. The ingredients used have unique qualities of being high in antioxidants and other soothing and disease preventing properties.

Dijon-Ginger Sauce has ginger which is a potent anti-nausea and anti-inflammatory herb. The pesto has fresh basil which is a cooling herb and rich in vitamin A and chlorophyll, a potent liver detoxifier. Pasta sauce, an age-old favorite, has tomatoes, which are rich in vitamin C and lycopene, a very potent antioxidant that reduces the risk for heart disease and cancer.

Dijon Ginger Sauce

Serves 10

1 cup plain non-fat greek yogurt
1 tbl Dijon mustard
1 tbl honey
1/2 tsp ginger powder

Directions:

Mix all ingredients together

Nutrient Analysis: cal 20

Exchanges: free

Sage-Butter Sauce

Serves 8

Cooking spray
3 tablespoons shallots, minced
4 ounces dry white wine
½ cup half & half
½ cup chicken broth, low-salt, divided
1 tablespoon lemon juice
1 tablespoon whipped butter, no added salt
3 tablespoons butter substitute granules
1 teaspoon cornstarch
1 teaspoon ground sage
½ teaspoon ground white pepper
½ teaspoon ground cayenne pepper

Directions:

1. Heat a small saucepan and coat with cooking spray; sauté shallots over medium-high heat until soft, 2-3 minutes.
2. Add wine, half & half, lemon juice and ¼ cup broth to saucepan. Simmer until reduced by half, 8-10 minutes.
3. Gradually, whisk in butter and butter substitute, stirring constantly. In a separate bowl, mix cornstarch with ¼ cup of broth then add to sauce.
4. Finish sauce with sage and seasonings. Keep warm in a water bath until ready to serve.

Nutrient Analysis: cal 51/pro 1/carb 4/fiber 0/fat 3/sodium 151

Exchanges: 1 fat

Adapted from Cuisine At Home Magazine

Duck Sauce for Chinese Food

Serves 12

½ cup apricot preserves
6 tablespoons water
2 teaspoons soy sauce, lower-sodium
1½ tablespoons apple cider vinegar
⅛ teaspoon garlic powder
1 medium apple, peeled, cored, chopped, cooked until tender
¾ cup canned lite and drained peaches, pears or pineapple, chopped
or fresh fruit, chopped
and cooked until tender

Directions:

4. Cook apricot preserves, water, soy sauce, vinegar and garlic powder
   until preserves melt.
5. Add apple and cook 5 minutes.
6. Add chopped fruit; mash and refrigerate

Nutrient Analysis: cal 49/pro 0/carb 13/fiber 0/fat 0/sodium 47

Exchanges: 1 fruit

Spaghetti Sauce

Serves 16

3 tablespoons olive oil
¼ cup onion, finely chopped
¼ cup green bell pepper, finely chopped
2 cloves garlic, finely chopped
1 - 12 ounce can tomatoes, no added salt
2 - 8 ounce cans tomato sauce, no added salt
1 - 6 ounce can tomato paste, no salt
½ teaspoon ground black pepper
½ teaspoon oregano
½ teaspoon basil
2 teaspoon sugar

Directions:

1. In a non-stick skillet heat oil and sauté onion, green pepper and garlic about 10 minutes.
2. Add canned tomatoes, sauce, paste, and spices. Stir with wooden spoon to break up tomatoes.
3. Over medium heat, bring mixture to just boiling; reduce heat and simmer uncovered for 20 minutes or until slightly thickened.

Nutrient Analysis: cal 54/pro 1/carb 7/fiber 1/fat 3/sodium 77

Exchanges: 1 veg, ½ fat

Pesto

Serves 12

1½ cups fresh basil
2 cloves garlic
2 tablespoons pine nuts
2 tablespoons olive oil
¾ cup chicken broth, fat-free, less-sodium
½ cup parmesan cheese, grated, reduced-fat

Directions:

1. Process all ingredients in a food processor until smooth.

Nutrient Analysis: cal 52/pro 1/carb 3/fiber 0/fat 4/sodium 104

Exchanges: 1 fat

Sweet 'N Sour Sauce for Chinese Food

Serves 4

2 tablespoons apple cider vinegar
1 tablespoon soy sauce, lower-sodium
¼ cup chicken broth, fat-free, less-sodium
1 tablespoon cornstarch
⅛ teaspoon garlic powder

Directions:

1. Mix all ingredients and pour over stir-fry. Toss until coated and mixture turns translucent.

Nutrient Analysis: cal 15/pro 1/carb 2/fiber 0/fat 0/sodium 204

Exchanges: free

Poultry

Poultry, including white meat chicken and turkey, are naturally lower in saturated fat than beef, but are akin to pork loin. Poultry may be easier to digest for some individuals who are sensitive to all fats. The saturated fat content for 3 ounces is only .9mg.

Poultry is high in Tryptophan, an amino acid that is the precursor to Serotonin, a neurotransmitter (brain chemical), that affects mood and appetite.

Niacin, a B vitamin that is important for energy production and a healthy cardiovascular system is abundant in poultry, 57% DV.

Again, grass fed and antibiotic-hormone free poultry offers the best nutritional advantage for this lean meat.

Cashew Chicken Salad

Serves 4

1 cup pineapple, chunk, in its own juice
8 ounces chicken breast, cooked, shredded
¼ cup scallions, chopped
1 ounce raw cashews (approx. 2 tablespoons)
½ cup fat-free Greek yogurt, plain
1 tablespoons olive oil
1 tablespoon wine vinegar
2 teaspoons soy sauce, low-sodium
1 cup salad greens

Directions:

1. Cut pineapple in half lengthwise through the crown. Refrigerate ½ hour.
2. Remove fruit from shell, leaving shell intact. Cut fruit into chunks.
3. Combine pineapple, chicken, scallions, and cashews. Spoon back into shell.
4. Combine yogurt, oil, vinegar, and soy sauce. Serve over salad.

Nutrient Analysis: cal 217/pro 22/carb 13/fiber 1/fat 9/sodium 112

Exchanges: 3 meat, 1 bread, 1½ fat

Make it a Meal: Serve with half-piece millet and flax lavash (toasted, if desired) and steamed asparagus.

Chicken Souvlaki

Serves 4

⅓ cup low-fat feta cheese, crumbled
½ cup fat-free Greek yogurt, plain
1 tablespoon fresh dill, chopped
1 teaspoon olive oil
1¼ teaspoons fresh garlic, minced, divided
Cooking spray
½ teaspoon dried oregano
2 cups boneless chicken breast, roasted, sliced
4 mini whole wheat pita bread
1 cup iceberg lettuce, shredded
½ cup cucumber, peeled, chopped
1 plum tomato, chopped
¼ cup red onion, sliced

Directions:

1. Combine feta cheese, yogurt, dill, 1 teaspoon olive oil, and ¼ teaspoon garlic in a small bowl, stirring well.
2. Heat large skillet over medium-high heat and coat with cooking spray.
3. Add remaining 1 teaspoon garlic and oregano to pan; sauté for 20 seconds.
4. Add chicken and cook for 2 minutes or until thoroughly heated.
5. Place ¼ cup chicken mixture in each pita half and top with 2 tablespoons yogurt mixture, 2 tablespoons shredded lettuce, 1 tablespoon cucumber, and 1 tablespoon tomato. Lastly, divide onion evenly among pitas and serve.

Nutrient Analysis: cal 248/pro 30/carb 17/fiber 3/fat 6/sodium 388

Exchanges: 4 meat, 1 bread, 1 fat

Make It A Meal: serve with ½ serving of Terra Chips

Adapted from Cooking Light Magazine (December 2007)

Grilled Chicken with Corn

and Black Bean Salsa

Serves 4

Salsa:
½ cup frozen corn, thawed
1 - 7½ ounce can black beans
½ cup red bell pepper, chopped
½ avocado
1 tablespoon pickled jalapeno, chopped
1 tablespoon dried cilantro (or 3 tablespoons fresh)
2 tablespoons lime juice
Chicken:
1 teaspoon ground black pepper
½ teaspoon chili powder
12 ounces boneless chicken breast
Cooking spray

Directions:

1. Combine salsa ingredients in medium bowl and set aside.
2. Combine black pepper and chili powder in a small bowl and sprinkle evenly over chicken pieces.
3. Coat grill pan with cooking spray and heat over medium high heat until hot.
4. Cook chicken 4 minutes on each side or until cooked through.
5. Spoon salsa over chicken.

Nutrient Analysis: cal 212/pro 25/carb 18/fiber 7/fat 5/sodium 269

Exchanges: 3 meat, 1 bread, 1 fat

Make it a Meal: Serve with 1 cup *Jicama Salad* and corn tortilla – quartered and baked until wedges are toasted.

Adapted from Diabetic Cooking

Oriental Chicken-Rice Bake

Serves 4

10 ounces cooked chicken, cubed
1 cup celery, diced
½ cup onion, diced
1 cup brown rice, cooked
3 tablespoons mayonnaise, fat-free
1 cup mushrooms, minced
1 teaspoon fresh lemon juice
10.75 ounce can cream of chicken soup, 98% fat-free
1 can water chestnuts, sliced
Topping:
½ cup Chinese noodles, (Chow Mein)
Cooking spray

Directions:

1. Preheat oven to 350°F. Grease a casserole dish.
2. Mix all ingredients except topping and spread into dish.
3. Crush noodles and sprinkle on top. Spray with cooking spray and bake for 35 minutes.

Nutrient Analysis: cal 293/pro 21/carb 33/fiber 4/fat 8/sodium 486

Exchanges: 3 meat, 2 bread, 1½ fat

Make it a Meal: For each serving add 1 cup steamed sugar snap peas tossed with ½ teaspoon sesame oil and a sprinkle of sesame seeds.

Prosciutto and Fontina Stuffed Chicken Breasts

Serves 4

1 ounce prosciutto, diced
1½ teaspoons dried rosemary
2 cloves garlic
¼ cup fontina cheese, shredded
4 - 4 ounce boneless chicken breasts, pounded thin
2 large egg whites
1 tablespoon Dijon mustard
¼ cup flour
¼ cup yellow cornmeal
Cooking spray

Directions:

1. Heat a large non-stick skillet over medium high heat; coat with cooking spray.
2. Add prosciutto to pan and sauté 2 minutes or until browned; add rosemary and garlic and sauté 1 minute.
3. Spoon prosciutto mixture into a bowl and cool to room temperature.
4. Stir in fontina cheese; set aside.
5. Stuff 2 tablespoons of the prosciutto mixture into each breast and roll.
6. Combine egg whites and mustard in a shallow dish, stirring mixture with a whisk.
7. Working with one chicken breast half at a time, dredge chicken in flour, shaking off excess.
8. Dip chicken into egg white mixture, allowing excess to drip off.
9. Coat chicken completely with cornmeal. Set aside.
10. Repeat sequence with remaining chicken, flour, egg mixture, and cornmeal. Let breasts set for 15-20 minutes.
11. Heat pan over medium-high heat; spray with cooking spray.

12. Add chicken to pan and reduce heat to medium. Cook 10 minutes on each side or until browned and white throughout chicken.

Nutrient Analysis: cal 233/pro 33/carb 13/fiber 2/fat 5/sodium 438

Exchanges: 5 meat, 1 bread, 1 fat

Make it a meal: Crisp green salad with 1/4 apple, chopped, tossed with 1 teaspoon oil and kosher salt and 1/3 cup cooked wheat berries.

Adapted from Cooking Light Magazine (December 2008)

Chicken Normandy

Serves 4

Cooking spray
2 tablespoons onion, chopped
¾ cup mushrooms, finely chopped
3 slices bread, dried, crumbled
2 tablespoons reduced-fat parmesan cheese, grated
¼ teaspoon ground black pepper
4 – 4 ounce boneless chicken breasts, pounded thin

Directions:

1. Spray skillet and sauté onions and mushrooms over medium heat.
2. Crumble bread and add to mushroom mixture with parmesan cheese and pepper.
3. Place stuffing in center of chicken and fold up sides of chicken, fastening with skewers or string. Chill.
4. Heat non-stick skillet over medium-high and coat with cooking spray.
5. Brown rolled chicken on all sides.
6. Remove to baking pan and bake at 350°F for 45 minutes.

Nutrient Analysis: cal 212/pro 28/carb 12/fiber 1/fat 4/sodium 246

Exchanges: 4 meat, 1 bread, 1 fat

Make it a meal: Add 1 serving *Broccoli Sunburst* and 1/4 cup cooked wild rice.

Crusted Chicken Breasts

Serves 4

4 boneless chicken breasts
Cooking spray
For dipping mixture:
2 large egg whites
2 teaspoons cornstarch
1 tablespoon fresh lemon juice
For crusting mixture:
1 cup coarse bread crumbs
1 tablespoon fresh parsley, chopped
1 dash kosher salt
¼ teaspoon ground black pepper
1 teaspoon lemon zest, minced

Directions:

1. Preheat oven to 450°F.
2. Prepare chicken breasts by cutting breasts in half and pounding to an even ½ inch thick.
3. In a wide, shallow dish blend egg whites, cornstarch, and lemon juice; set aside.
4. Combine bread crumbs, parsley, salt, pepper, and zest in a second wide, shallow dish.
5. Crust chicken breasts by dipping a chicken breast into the egg mixture, letting the excess run off, then fully coating in bread crumb mixture. Repeat for each chicken breast.
6. Let chicken rest at room temperature on a rack for 20 minutes to set crust.
7. Using a large, nonstick oven-proof skillet, coat with cooking spray and sauté chicken over moderate-high heat for about 3 minutes or until golden-brown and crisp, turning to crisp both sides.

8. Carefully turn with a spatula and transfer skillet to oven for about 8 minutes until chicken is done.

Nutrient Analysis: cal 152/pro 23/carb 9/fiber1/fat 2/sodium 189

Exchanges: 3 meat, ½ bread, ½ fat

Alternatives:
  ➤ Parmesan Crusted Chicken: Add ¼ cup grated parmesan cheese to crusting mixture.

Make it a meal: 1 serving *Sage-Butter Sauce*, 1 serving *Roasted Potatoes with Garlic and Rosemary*, ½ cup steamed green beans.

Adapted from Cuisine At Home Magazine

Mexican Casserole with Tortilla Chips

Serves 4

Cooking spray
¾ pound ground turkey breast, lean
½ cup canned black beans, drained & rinsed
8 ounce bag frozen red & green pepper strips
14½ ounce can stewed tomatoes, no salt added
¾ teaspoon ground cumin
¼ cup low-fat cheddar cheese, finely shredded
1½ ounces low-fat tortilla chips, unsalted

Directions:

1. Place large, non-stick skillet over medium-high heat until hot. Coat with cooking spray.
2. Add turkey. Cook, stirring to break up meat until no longer pink.
3. Add beans, pepper strips, tomatoes, and cumin. Bring to a boil. Reduce heat, cover, and simmer for 20 minutes or until vegetables are tender.
4. Remove from heat, sprinkle evenly with cheese and serve with tortilla chips.

Nutrient Analysis: cal 270/pro 22/carb 24/fiber 4/fat 10/sodium 163

Exchanges: 3 meat, 2 fat, 1 bread, 1 vegetable

Make it a Meal: Enjoy with a *Simple Side Salad*.

Adapted from Diabetic Cooking

Pasta with Chicken, Spinach and Ricotta

Serves 4

4 ounces Rotini pasta, tri-colored
Cooking spray
1 box (10 ounce) frozen chopped spinach, thawed, squeezed dry
2 teaspoons fresh garlic, minced
1 cup cooked chicken, diced
1 cup ricotta cheese, non-fat
¼ cup mozzarella cheese, part-skim, shredded
2 tablespoons grated parmesan cheese, divided
½ cup water
½ teaspoon chicken bouillon
½ teaspoon ground black pepper

Directions:

1. Cook pasta according to package directions, omitting salt. Drain.
2. While pasta is cooking, coat skillet with non-stick cooking spray. Heat over medium-high heat. Add spinach and garlic; cook and stir 3 minutes. Add chicken and cook another 2 minutes.
3. Stir in ricotta, mozzarella, 1 tablespoon parmesan cheese, water, bouillon and pepper.
4. Drain pasta and add to skillet; stir until well blended. Sprinkle with remaining parmesan cheese and serve.

Nutrient Analysis: cal 273/pro 25/carb 30/fiber 3/fat 5/sodium 239

Exchanges: 3 meat, 2 bread, 1 fat

Make it a Meal: Serve with 1 cup steamed sliced carrots.

Adapted from Diabetic Cooking

Spicy Chicken Sandwiches with Cilantro-Lime Mayo

Serves 4

Chill Time: 2 – 8 hours

Mayo Ingredients:

2 tablespoons mayonnaise, reduced-fat
2 tablespoons plain Greek yogurt, fat-free
2 tablespoons fresh cilantro or 2 teaspoons dried
1 teaspoon fresh lime juice
1 clove garlic, minced

Chicken ingredients:

¼ cup egg substitute
3 tablespoons hot pepper sauce
1 teaspoon dried oregano
12 ounces boneless chicken breast
1½ ounces tortilla chips, baked w/less oil - crushed
Cooking spray

Sandwich ingredients:

4 slices onion
4 leafs iceberg lettuce
2 pieces Millet & Flax Lavash (or use mini pitas)

Directions:

1. To prepare mayo, combine the first 5 ingredients.
2. For the chicken, combine egg substitute, hot sauce, and oregano in a large zip-top plastic bag.
3. Cut chicken breast halves in half to form 4 cutlets.
4. Add chicken to bag; seal. Marinate in refrigerator at least 2 hours or up to 8 hours, turning bag occasionally.
5. Place tortilla chips in food processor; process 1 minute or until ground. Place chips in shallow dish.

6. Working with one cutlet at a time, remove chicken from marinade, allowing excess to drip off.
7. Coat chicken completely in chips and set aside. Repeat procedure with each cutlet.
8. Heat large non-stick skillet over medium heat; coat with cooking spray.
9. Add chicken to pan; cook 3 minutes on each side or until browned and done.
10. Cut each piece of Lavash into quarters. Assemble sandwich by spreading mayo evenly on Lavash; add chicken, onion and lettuce if desired.

Nutrient Analysis: cal 252/pro 27/carb 24/fiber 6/fat 5/sodium 486

Exchanges: 4 meat, 1 bread, 1 fat

Make it a meal: Serve with additional chopped greens, tomatoes and cucumbers drizzled with lime juice and 1 teaspoon olive oil.
Adapted from Cooking Light Magazine (December 2008)

Chicken Picatta

Serves 5

1 egg
5 tablespoons fresh lemon juice, divided
¼ cup flour
½ teaspoon garlic powder
½ teaspoon paprika
1 tablespoon butter, no added salt
1 pound chicken cutlets
1 cup chicken broth, non-fat, lower-sodium
8 capers

Directions:

1. Beat egg with 1 tablespoon lemon juice.
2. In a separate, shallow bowl combine flour, garlic and paprika.
3. Heat butter in a skillet.
4. Dip each cutlet in egg then in flour mixture. Brown in skillet.
5. Add chicken broth, remaining lemon juice and capers to skillet.
6. Cover and simmer 2 minutes.

Nutrient Analysis: cal 172/pro 24/carb 7/fiber 1/fat 5/sodium 111

Exchanges: 3 meat, ½ bread, 1 fat

Make it a meal: Add 1 cup steamed broccoli, ½ cup cooked wild rice, and ½ tablespoon butter.

Adapted from Julie Edgar

Grilled Chicken Skewers

Serves 6

1 pound boneless chicken breast
Simple Asian master marinade:
2 tablespoons soy sauce, low sodium
1 tablespoon rice vinegar
½ teaspoon sesame oil
½ teaspoon olive oil

Directions:

1. Rinse chicken; drain and cut into 1-inch cubes. Put in bowl with all of the marinade ingredients. Toss lightly to coat.
2. Soak bamboo skewers in water to cover for 10 minutes.
3. Thread the chicken cubes onto the skewers, leaving a half-inch on each end.
4. Prepare a medium-hot fire for grilling or preheat gas grill or broiler. If grilling, brush the rack with olive oil and place meat 3 inches from heat source.
5. Grill covered or broil 5 - 7 minutes per side, or until chicken is opaque all the way through.

Nutrient Analysis: cal 151/pro 25/carb 1/fiber 0/fat 4/sodium 160

Exchanges: 4 meat, 1 fat

Make it a Meal: Serve with ½ serving *Grilled Garlic Naan, Asian Slaw* and 2 tablespoons Edamame (soybeans).

Adapted from Nina Simonds, Whole Foods Market InSeason (2007)

Orange Chicken Stir-Fry over Quinoa

Serves 4

1 pound boneless chicken breast, cut into chunks
Cooking spray
1 cup water
½ cup quinoa
1 tablespoon cornstarch
1 cup orange juice
1 tablespoon soy sauce, low sodium
2 tablespoons ginger root, grated
½ cup green onion, sliced
1 cup carrot, sliced
12 ounces snow peas, ends trimmed
1 cup sweet red pepper, sliced

Directions:

1. Heat skillet over medium-high heat and lightly coat with cooking spray.
2. Add chicken; cook and stir 4-6 minutes or until centers of chicken are no longer pink. Remove from skillet and keep warm.
3. Meanwhile, place water and quinoa in medium saucepan; bring to boil.
4. Reduce to simmer, cover and cook until all water is absorbed, about 12-15 minutes.
5. Whisk together cornstarch, orange juice and soy sauce; add to skillet. Bring to simmer, stirring frequently.
6. Add ginger and onion, stirring constantly, about 1-2 minutes. Add carrots, snow peas and red peppers. Simmer 3-4 minutes uncovered until carrots are crisp-tender.
7. Return chicken to skillet; heat about 1 or 2 minutes until heated through. Let stand about 4 minutes uncovered for flavors to set in.
8. Serve chicken mixture over quinoa.

Nutrient Analysis: cal 303/pro 32/carb 35/fiber 5/fat 3/sodium 178

Exchanges: 5 meat, 2 bread, ½ fat

A meal within itself! Enjoy!

Adapted from Diabetic Cooking

Pecan Crusted Chicken

Serves 4

12 ounces boneless chicken breasts
Cooking spray
For Dipping Mixture:
2 large egg whites
2 teaspoons cornstarch
1 tablespoon fresh lemon juice
For Crusting Mixture:
1 cup bread crumbs
1 tablespoon fresh parsley, chopped
½ cup pecans, finely chopped
½ teaspoon dried oregano
½ teaspoon dried thyme
½ teaspoon paprika
½ teaspoon ground cayenne pepper
¼ teaspoon ground black pepper
1 teaspoon lemon zest, minced

Directions:

1. Preheat oven to 450°F.
2. Prepare chicken breasts by cutting breasts in half and pounding to an even ½ inch thick.
3. In a wide, shallow dish blend egg whites, cornstarch, and lemon juice with a fork; set aside.
4. Combine crusting mixture ingredients in a second shallow dish.
5. Crust chicken breasts by dipping a chicken breast into the egg mixture, letting the excess run off, then fully coating in bread crumb mixture. Repeat for each chicken breast.
6. Let chicken rest at room temperature on a rack for 20 minutes to set crust.

7. Using a large, nonstick oven-proof skillet, coat with cooking spray and sauté chicken over moderate-high heat for about 3 minutes or until golden-brown and crisp, turning to crisp both sides.
8. Carefully turn with a spatula and transfer skillet to oven for about 8 minutes until chicken is done.

Nutrient Analysis: cal 242/pro 24/carb 10/fiber 2/fat 12/sodium 150

Exchanges: 3 meat, ½ bread, 2 fat

Make it a Meal: 1 cup steamed broccoli, ½ cup *Roasted Potatoes with Garlic & Rosemary*

Adapted from Cuisine At Home Magazine

Tuscan Turkey and White Bean Skillet

Serves 6

1 teaspoon dried rosemary, divided
½ teaspoon garlic powder
½ teaspoon black pepper, divided
1 pound turkey breast cutlets
Cooking spray
14½ ounce can fire roasted tomatoes, diced, undrained
16 ounce can navy beans, no salt added, drained and rinsed
¼ cup parmesan cheese, grated, reduced fat

Directions:

1. In a small bowl, combine ½ teaspoon rosemary, garlic powder and ¼ teaspoon pepper; mix well and sprinkle over cutlets.
2. Heat pan over medium-high and coat with cooking spray.
3. Add half of cutlets; cook 2–3 minutes per side or until no longer pink in center.
4. Transfer to serving platter and tent with foil to keep warm. Repeat with remaining cutlets.
5. Add tomatoes with their juices, beans, remaining rosemary and pepper to same skillet; bring to boil over high heat. Reduce heat; simmer 5 minutes.
6. Spoon tomato mixture over and around cutlets on serving platter and top evenly with cheese.

Nutrient Analysis: cal 221/pro 22/carb 16/fiber 5/fat 6/sodium 258

Exchanges: 3 meat, 1 bread, 1 fat

Make it a Meal: Serve over ⅓ cup millet with 1 cup of steamed green beans or pole beans.

Adapted from Diabetic Cooking

Turkey Burgers

Serves 6

1 pound ground turkey breast
1 large egg white
¼ cup bread crumbs
½ teaspoon dry mustard powder
½ teaspoon dried basil
½ teaspoon dried oregano
½ teaspoon dried parsley
1 teaspoon Worcestershire sauce
¼ teaspoon garlic powder
Cooking spray
6 wheat English muffins, toasted
6 inner-leafs red leaf lettuce
6 thin-slices tomato
6 slices onion

Directions:

1. Mix all ingredients.
2. Form 6 burger patties from the meat mixture.
3. Coat skillet with cooking spray and sauté burgers until cooked through.

Nutrient Analysis: cal 270/pro 21/carb 30/fiber 5/fat 8/sodium 506

Exchanges: 3 meat, 2 bread, 1½ fat

Make it a Meal:
Serve with 1 cup *Coleslaw* and about 5 baby carrots.

Pork

Pork, also known as the "other white meat" or earlier known as the meat made from scraps and garbage, has nutritional advantages and although it is actually a red meat, it is as lean as white meat chicken and turkey.

Pork is abundant in iron, offering 105%DV! Iron is essential for the proper functioning of hemoglobin thus allowing oxygen to be transported from the lungs to the tissues in the body.

Selenium, a mineral needed for glutathione production (a powerful antioxidant in the body) and DNA repair in damaged cells, is found in abundance in pork, 60% DV.

Phosphorus is a mineral that is involved in skeletal tissue as well as tooth formation and other functions. Pork provides 24% DV for this mineral.

Variety in flesh proteins offers advantages as each animal has different "star" nutrients.

.

Asian-Style Meatloaf Muffins

Serves 6

1 ounce brown rice crackers, wheat-free
¾ pound ground turkey breast
½ pound ground pork, lean
½ cup green onions, chopped
2 tablespoons Hoisin sauce
½ cup red bell pepper, chopped
¼ cup canned Chinese water chestnuts, drained, chopped
2 tablespoons soy sauce, lower sodium, wheat-free
2 teaspoons fresh ginger root, grated
2 cloves garlic, minced
2 large egg whites
Cooking spray

Directions:

1. Preheat oven to 350°F.
2. Place crackers in food processor; process until finely chopped.
3. Combine cracker crumbs, turkey, pork, green onions and remaining ingredients except cooking spray in large bowl.
4. Grease muffin tin with cooking spray. Spoon meat mixture into 12 muffin cups. Top each with 1 teaspoon Hoisin sauce.
5. Bake for 45 minutes or until a thermometer registers 165°F. Let stand 5 minutes before serving.

Nutrient Analysis: cal 200/pro 20/carb 11/fiber 1/fat 8/sodium 352

Exchanges: 3 meat, 1 bread, 1½ fat

Make it a meal: Serve with *Asian Slaw* and ½ serving *Crispy Spiced Almond Wontons* OR *Braised Bok Choy* and 1/4 cup cooked brown rice.

Adapted from Cooking Light Magazine

Pork Tabbouleh

Serves 6

Chill Time: 2 hours

1 cup dry bulgur
1½ cups boiling water
1½ cups (approx. 8 ounces) *Simply Roasted Pork Tenderloin*, cubed
2 cups plum tomatoes, seeded, chopped
1 cup cucumber, seeded, chopped
1 cup fresh parsley, chopped
½ cup green onion, chopped
½ cup fresh mint leaf
1 - 15½ ounce can garbanzo beans (chickpeas), low sodium
Dressing ingredients:
⅓ cup fresh lemon juice (approx. 2 lemons)
1 tablespoon olive oil
¼ teaspoon ground black pepper
1 clove garlic, minced

Directions:

1. Combine water and bulgur in a large bowl; cover and let stand 15 minutes or until water is absorbed and bulgur is tender.
2. Add *Simply Roasted Pork* and next 6 ingredients; toss gently to combine.
3. Combine lemon juice and remaining ingredients, stirring with a whisk. Drizzle juice mixture over pork mixture; toss to combine.
4. Chill at least 2 hours before serving.

Recipe Nutrient Analysis: cal 230/pro 21/carb 31/fiber 8/fat 6/sodium 167

Exchanges: 3 meat, 1 bread, 1 vegetable, 1 fat

Make it a Meal: Serve with homemade *Pita Crisps.*
Adapted from Cooking Light Magazine

Warm Spinach Salad with Pork and Pears

Serves 4

Pork Ingredients:
Cooking spray
1 pound pork tenderloin, trimmed, cut into 12 slices
1 dash salt, kosher
⅛ teaspoon ground black pepper

Dressing ingredients:
3 tablespoons water
3 tablespoons red wine vinegar
1 tablespoon olive oil
⅛ teaspoon ground black pepper

Salad ingredients:
1 cup (approx. 1) Anjou or Bartlett pear, thinly sliced
2 tablespoons golden raisins
2 - 5 ounce packages baby spinach
2 tablespoons blue cheese, crumbled

Directions:

1. Heat a large non-stick skillet over medium-high heat and coat with cooking spray.
2. Sprinkle pork evenly with a dash of salt and ⅛ teaspoon pepper. Add pork to pan; cook 4 minutes on each side or until browned.
3. Combine water, vinegar, oil and pepper in small bowl, stirring with a whisk.
4. Combine pear, raisins and spinach in a large bowl; toss well.
5. Arrange 2 cups spinach mixture on each of 4 plates and drizzle evenly with vinegar mixture.
6. Top each serving with 3 pork slices and 1½ teaspoons blue cheese.

Nutrient Analysis: cal 250/pro 27/carb 18/fiber 5/fat 9/sodium 272

Exchanges: 4 meat, 2 fat, ½ fruit, 1 vegetable

Make it a Meal: Serve with *Home Fried Sweet Potatoes.*
Adapted from Cooking Light Magazine, December 2008

Maple-Balsamic-Glazed Pork Medallions

Serves 4

2 tablespoons maple syrup
3 tablespoons balsamic vinegar
1 tablespoon prepared Dijon mustard
1 pound pork tenderloin
2 teaspoons olive oil
1 dash salt, kosher
¼ teaspoon ground black pepper

Directions:

1. In a small saucepan combine syrup and vinegar; bring to boil. Cook, stirring occasionally, for about 3 minutes until reduced.
2. Remove from heat and stir in mustard.
3. Cut pork crosswise into 8 pieces. Place each pork piece between 2 sheets of heavy-duty plastic wrap; pound to ¼-inch thickness using a meat mallet or small heavy skillet.
4. Heat oil in large non-stick skillet over medium-high heat.
5. Sprinkle pork evenly with salt and pepper. Add pork to pan; cook 3 minutes on each side.
6. Add vinegar mixture; cook 1 minute or until desired degree of doneness, turning pork to coat.
7. Place 2 pork medallions on each of 4 plates; drizzle remaining sauce from pan evenly onto each serving.

Nutrient Analysis: cal 190/pro 24/carb 9/fiber 0/fat 6/sodium 189

Exchanges: 3 meat, ½ bread, 1 fat

Make it a meal: Steamed broccoli and *Stove Top Home Fried Sweet Potatoes or Potatoes*

Adapted from Cooking Light Magazine

Pork Tenderloin with Avocado-Tomatillo Salsa

Serves 4

Pork Ingredients:
1½ teaspoons chili powder
½ teaspoon ground cumin
1 pound pork tenderloin
1 teaspoon olive oil

Salsa Ingredients:
2 medium tomatillos, shucked, diced
½ avocado, diced
1 Jalapeno pepper, seeded, finely chopped
1 clove garlic, minced
2 tablespoons red onion, finely chopped
1 tablespoon lime juice
1 tablespoon fresh cilantro, chopped

Directions:

1. Preheat oven to 425°F.
2. Combine chili powder and cumin in small bowl. Sprinkle evenly on pork, pressing to allow spices to adhere.
3. Heat oil in large nonstick skillet over medium-high heat; add pork and cook 3 minutes. Turn; cook 2 to 3 minutes longer or until richly browned.
4. Place meat on foil-lined baking sheet; bake 10 minutes, then reduce heat to 350°and cook for 45 minutes.
5. Remove from oven and let stand 5 minutes before slicing.
6. Combine salsa ingredients in small bowl and toss gently to blend. Serve with pork.

Nutrient Analysis: cal 191/pro 25/carb 5/fiber 3/fat 8/sodium 70

Exchanges: 3 meat, 1½ fat

Make it a Meal: For each serving, add 2½ cups crisp greens (such as romaine, arugula, spinach, radicchio, etc.) and a small, oven roasted sweet potato.

Adapted from Diabetic Cooking

Roasted Pork and Vegetable Salad

Serves 4

2 medium (approx. 3" diameter) red potatoes
1 large zucchini, cut lengthwise into ¼-inch-thick slices
1 large summer squash, cut lengthwise into ¼-inch-thick slices
1 large red bell pepper, quartered
1 large yellow/orange bell pepper, quartered
1 small red onion, cut into ¼-inch-thick slices
1 clove garlic, peeled, halved
2 teaspoons olive oil
2 cups (about 12 oz.) *Simply Roasted Pork Tenderloin*, thinly sliced
1 tablespoon plus 1 teaspoon white wine vinegar
1 tablespoon honey
1 teaspoon prepared Dijon mustard
1 teaspoon fresh oregano, chopped
½ teaspoon fresh thyme
¼ teaspoon ground black pepper

Directions:

1. Preheat oven to 400°F.
2. Place potatoes, vegetables, and garlic in a large plastic food storage bag. Drizzle olive oil into the bag. Seal tightly; shake to coat all vegetables.
3. Transfer vegetables to baking sheet. Oven roast for about 20 minutes; turn vegetables and roast another 5-10 minutes until fork tender.
4. Toss vegetables in large bowl with Simply Roasted Pork.
5. In a separate bowl, combine vinegar and remaining ingredients, stirring with a whisk.
6. Drizzle vinegar mixture over vegetable pork mixture, tossing to coat.

This dish may be served warm or cold.

Nutrient Analysis: cal 311/pro 29/carb 34/fiber 5/fat 7/sodium 98

Exchanges: 4 meat, 1 bread, 2 vegetable, 1 fat

Make it a Meal: Serve with ¼ cup *Sautéed Grains*
Adapted from Cooking Light Magazine

Rosemary Roast Pork Tenderloin & Vegetables

Serves 6

¼ cup chicken broth, non-fat, lower sodium
1 teaspoon olive oil
Cooking spray
3 parsnips, peeled, cut diagonally into ½-inch slices
3 medium carrots
1 medium red bell pepper, cut into ¾-inch pieces
1 medium green bell pepper, cut into ¾-inch pieces
1 medium onion, sweet or yellow, cut into wedges
2 – 12 ounce loins pork tenderloin
2 tablespoons Dijon mustard or hot Dijon mustard
2 teaspoons dried rosemary
½ teaspoon ground black pepper

Directions:

1. Preheat oven to 450°F.
2. In a small bowl, combine broth and oil.
3. Coat large shallow roasting pan or jelly roll pan with non-stick cooking spray. Add parsnips and carrots; sprinkle with 3 tablespoons broth mixture. Bake 10 minutes.
4. Add bell peppers, onion and remaining broth mixture to roasting pan; toss to coat.
5. Push vegetables to perimeter of pan. Place tenderloins in center of pan; spread mustard over tenderloins. Sprinkle rosemary and black pepper over meat and vegetables.
6. Bake 10 minutes, then reduce temperature to 350°. Remove vegetables after 30 minutes and finish pork for 15 minutes longer.
7. Transfer tenderloins to carving board; tent with foil and let stand 5 minutes.
8. Carve tenderloins crosswise into ½-inch slices; serve with vegetables and any juices from pan.

Nutrient Analysis: cal 234/pro 26/carb 21/fiber 5/fat 5/sodium 210

Exchanges: 4 meat, 1 bread, 1 fat

Make it a meal: 1 serving mashed potatoes (6 servings = 3 large pota-toes, mashed; ¼ cup milk; 1 teaspoon butter substitute granules).

Adapted from Diabetic Cooking

Simply Roasted Pork Tenderloin

Serves 4

1 pound pork tenderloin
1 teaspoon olive oil

Rub Options:
½ teaspoon garlic powder
1 teaspoon rosemary

¼ teaspoon onion powder
½ teaspoon chili powder
½ teaspoon cumin

1 teaspoon apricot all-fruit conserve
½ teaspoon thyme
1 teaspoon soy sauce

Directions:

1. Preheat oven to 450°.
2. Rub pork loin with oil.
3. Rub loin with one of the options listed above.
4. Place loin on baking rack in pan and bake in oven at 450° for 10 minutes.
5. Reduce heat to 350°and continue roasting for 50 minutes longer.
6. Remove from oven and let stand 10 minutes before slicing.

Nutrient Analysis: cal 163/pro 29/carb 0/fiber 0/fat 4/sodium 64

Exchanges: 4 meat, 1 fat

Note: Pork loin freezes well and can be used in stir-fries, salads, etc.

Beef

Beef has many nutritional benefits that have been overlooked now for many years since the cholesterol revolution. While excessive consumption of animal protein is undesirable, the portions outlined in this book (approximately 3-4 ounces or 100 grams), one to three times per week, can provide nutrients that we now often take in pill or supplement form.

Lean red meat is found in the round cuts of the beef: eye of round, top and bottom round - since this is the most muscular area of the animal.

Cattle were not designed to eat grains, corn and soy, thus much of the meat consumed in this country is high in saturated fat and lower in omega three fatty acids. Grass-fed meat, on the other hand, can have a much higher omega three content and it is usually lower in saturated fat.

Lean red meats offer exceptional vitamin B12 content, upwards of 49% DV (daily value). Zinc is another mineral found in abundant quantity and zinc is important to maintain healthy blood vessel walls thus keeping the cardiovascular system healthy. Lean beef has 34% DV for zinc.

While variety is the best way to ensure obtaining adequate nutrition, lean beef can be included in a healthy diet.

Beef Stroganoff

Serves 6

½ tablespoon extra virgin olive oil
1¼ pounds beef flank steak, cut into thin strips
1 cup mushrooms, sliced
1 medium onion, sliced
1 cube or 1 teaspoon beef bouillon, low sodium
1 cup hot water
1 tablespoon ketchup, no added salt
½ tablespoon yellow mustard
1 tablespoon flour
¼ cup cold water
½ cup plain, fat-free Greek yogurt

Directions:

1. In a large pan, heat olive oil and cook steak, mushrooms, and onions. Add bouillon, 1 cup of hot water, ketchup, and mustard. Cover and simmer 30 minutes or until tender.
2. Combine flour and water. Stir into meat mixture. Cook, stirring constantly, until mixture comes to a boil.
3. Reduce heat and stir in yogurt until heated through.

Nutrient Analysis: cal 170/pro 23/carb 5/fiber 0/fat 6/sodium 178

Exchanges: 3 meat, 1 fat

Make it a Meal: Serve over ½ cup of whole wheat egg noodles with 1 serving of *Honey Roasted Root Vegetables*

Italian Style Meatloaf

Serves 6

1 ½ pounds ground beef, 95% lean
1 cup pasta sauce, tomato & basil, light
½ cup bread crumbs
⅓ cup parmesan cheese, shredded
½ cup onion, finely chopped
⅓ cup fresh parsley, flat-leaf
1 teaspoon garlic powder
½ teaspoon dried basil
½ teaspoon dried oregano
¼ teaspoon ground black pepper
2 large egg whites
Cooking spray

Directions:

6. Preheat oven to 350°F.
7. In a large bowl, combine beef, ½ cup pasta sauce and remaining ingredients except cooking spray.
8. Place beef mixture into an 8 x 4-inch loaf pan coated with cooking spray. Brush remaining ½ cup pasta sauce on top of meatloaf.
9. Bake for 1 hour and 10 minutes.
10. Let stand 10 minutes then cut into 12 slices.

Nutrient Analysis: cal 219/pro 29/carb 7/fiber 1/fat 8/sodium 323

Exchanges: 4 meat, ½ bread, 1½ fat

Make it a Meal: Serve with 1 small baked potato, ½ cup steamed broccoli & ½ cup steamed cauliflower.

Adapted from Cooking Light Magazine

Creamy Baked Hamburger Casserole

Serves 6

5 ounces elbow macaroni
Cooking spray
3/4 pound ground beef, 95% lean
8 ounces tomato sauce, divided
½ cup cottage cheese, 1% fat, no added salt
2 ounces low-fat cream cheese
⅓ cup scallions, minced
1 tablespoon green bell pepper, minced
¼ cup plain, fat-free Greek yogurt

Directions:

1. Preheat oven to 350°F.
2. Cook and drain macaroni.
3. Meanwhile, scramble hamburger as it browns in a skillet. Drain fat if necessary; then add one tablespoon tomato sauce.
4. In a bowl, combine cottage and cream cheese, scallions, and green pepper.
5. Coat casserole dish with cooking spray and add half of the macaroni to the dish. Cover with the cheese mixture and add rest of macaroni.
6. Spread meat mixture into dish then top with yogurt and remainder of tomato sauce.
7. Bake for 45 minutes and let stand 10 minutes before serving.

Nutrient Analysis: cal 227/pro 21/carb 21/fiber 1/fat 5/sodium 295

Exchanges: 3 meat, 1 1/2 bread, 1 fat

Make it a Meal: Serve with a *Simple Side Salad* and half piece of Millet & Flax Lavash, toasted if desired.

Canelloni

Serves 6

¾ pound ground beef, 95% lean
½ medium onion, chopped
5 ounces frozen, chopped spinach
2 ounces non-fat mozzarella, shredded
¼ cup bread crumbs
1 medium egg, slightly beaten
½ teaspoon dried oregano
¼ teaspoon ground black pepper
4 tablespoons grated parmesan cheese, divided
½ pound whole wheat lasagna noodles
2 cups tomato sauce

Directions:

1. Preheat oven to 350°F.
2. Sauté hamburger (or use ground turkey if you prefer) and onion; pour off fat.
3. Add spinach mozzarella, bread crumbs, egg, oregano, pepper and 2 tablespoons parmesan cheese.
4. Cook lasagna noodles and cut in half widthwise.
5. Put 1 cup of sauce on bottom of pan. Place filling in each pasta strip and roll. Set in pan, seam side down.
6. Pour rest of sauce over rolls and sprinkle with remaining parmesan cheese. Cover with foil and bake 25 minutes. Uncover the last 5 minutes and let set 5 minutes before serving.

Nutrient Analysis: cal 300/pro 26/carb 35/fiber 8/fat 6/sodium 548

Exchanges: 5 meat, 2 bread, 1 fat
Make It A Meal: serve with a *Simple Salad*.

Meatloaf "Muffins"

Serves 8 (2 "muffins" each)

Cooking spray
1 cup onion, finely chopped
½ cup carrot, finely chopped
1 teaspoon dried oregano
2 cloves garlic, minced
¾ cup ketchup, no added salt
1½ pounds ground beef, 95% lean
1 cup (18 - 20 crackers) Saltine crackers, non-fat, finely crushed
2 tablespoons yellow mustard, prepared
1 teaspoon Worcestershire sauce
¼ teaspoon ground black pepper
2 eggs
Cooking spray

Directions:

1. Preheat oven to 350°F.
2. Coat large non-stick skillet with cooking spray over medium-high heat. Add chopped onion, carrot, dried oregano, and minced garlic. Sauté 2 minutes. Cool.
3. Combine onion mixture, 1/4 cup ketchup, and remaining ingredients except cooking spray in large bowl.
4. Coat muffin tin with cooking spray. Spoon meat mixture into 16 (2 inch) muffin tins. Top each with about 2 teaspoons of ketchup.
5. Bake for 25 minutes or until a thermometer registers 160°F. Let stand 5 minutes before serving.

Nutrient Analysis: cal 201/pro 21/carb 15/fiber 1/fat 5/sodium 270

Exchanges: 3 meat, 1 bread, 1 fat

Make it a meal: 1 serving (½ cup) *Roasted Butternut Squash with Rosemary* & 1 cup steamed green beans.
Adapted from Cooking Light Magazine

Thai-Style Beef with Pasta on Lettuce

Serves 6

¼ cup orange juice
2 tablespoons low-sodium creamy peanut butter or almond butter
3 tablespoons low-sodium soy sauce
1 tablespoon rice vinegar
1 tablespoon fresh ginger root, grated
7 ounces whole wheat spaghetti
1 pound ground beef, 95% lean
1 tablespoon garlic, minced
3 cups bok choy, thinly sliced
4 large carrots, coarsely chopped
4 small green onions, w/tops & bulb, bias-sliced into 1-inch pieces
½ teaspoon crushed red pepper
6 outer-leafs of lettuce
2 tablespoons almonds or peanuts, dry roasted, no salt

Directions:

1. In small food processor or blender combine orange juice, peanut butter, soy sauce, vinegar and ginger. Cover and process until nearly smooth. Set aside.
2. Cook spaghetti according to directions, drain and set aside.
3. Meanwhile, in large, non-stick skillet cook ground beef and garlic over medium heat until meat is brown. Drain off any fat.
4. Stir in bok choy, carrot, green onions, and red pepper. Drizzle with orange juice mixture. Reduce heat to medium. Cover and cook 2 minutes.
5. Add hot spaghetti. Toss until combined.
6. Place lettuce leaves on serving plates. Spoon mixture into leaves. Sprinkle with roasted nuts.

Nutrient Analysis: cal 317/pro 24/carb 33/fiber 5/fat 10/sodium 284

Exchanges: 3 meat, 2 bread, 2 fat, 1 vegetable
A meal in itself!
Adapted from Diabetic Cooking

Cumin-Pepper Flank Steak

with Horseradish Chimichurri

Recipe Note: *Chimichurri is a thick herb sauce*
for meat that is popular in Argentina

Serves 4

Chimichurri Ingredients:

⅔ cup fresh parsley
2 tablespoons green onion, chopped
2 tablespoon water
1 tablespoon prepared horseradish
1 tablespoon red wine vinegar
½ teaspoon olive oil
1 clove garlic, peeled

Steak Ingredients:

1 pound beef flank steak, trimmed
1 teaspoon ground cumin
1 dash salt
¼ teaspoon ground black pepper
Cooking spray

Directions:

1. To prepare chimichurri, combine first 8 ingredients in a food processor; process until smooth.
2. To prepare steak, rub steak with cumin, salt and pepper. Heat large non-stick skillet over medium-high heat and coat with cooking spray.
3. Add steak to pan; cook 3 minutes on each side or until desired degree of doneness.
4. Remove from pan; let stand 5 minutes. Cut steak diagonally across grain into thin slices. Serve with chimichurri.

Nutrient Analysis: cal 203/pro 25/carb 2/fiber 1/fat 10/sodium 121

Exchanges: 3½ meat, 2 fat

Make it a meal: Serve with 1 cup sliced carrots, steamed and ⅓ cup cooked brown rice.

Adapted from Cooking Light Magazine, December 2008

Mexi-Corn Lasagna

Serves 8

1 pound ground beef, 95% lean
15 ounce can corn, rinsed & drained
15 ounce can tomato sauce, no added salt
1 cup picante sauce
1 teaspoon chili powder
1 teaspoon cumin
16 ounces low-fat cottage cheese, no added salt
1 large egg, slightly beaten
¼ cup parmesan cheese, grated
1 teaspoon oregano
½ teaspoon garlic powder
6 corn tortillas, no added salt
4 ounces reduced-fat cheddar cheese

Directions:

1. Brown and drain ground beef (or turkey if you prefer). May also substitute 2 cups kidney beans for meat. Set aside.
2. Preheat oven to 375°F.
3. Combine next five ingredients in large skillet. Simmer 5 minutes, stirring frequently.
4. In a bowl combine cottage cheese, eggs, parmesan cheese, oregano, and garlic powder; mix well.
5. Lightly grease a 13 x 9 inch baking dish and arrange 4 tortillas on the bottom and sides of it, overlapping as necessary.
6. Top with half of the meat mixture. Spoon cheese mixture over meat. Arrange remaining tortilla over cheese. Top with remaining meat mixture.
7. Bake until hot and bubbly, about 30 minutes.
8. Remove from oven, sprinkle with cheddar cheese, and let stand 10 minutes before serving.

Nutrient Analysis: cal 306/pro 28/carb 27/fiber 3/fat 10/sodium 567

Exchanges: 4 meat, 1½ bread, 2 fat

Make it a Meal: Serve with 1 cup mixed greens (such as spinach, aru-gula, radicchio, romaine, etc.) and ⅓ cup shredded carrot.

Adapted from: PACE Picante Sauce

Fish and Shellfish

Most fish are low in total fat and calories and all fish are low in saturated fat, thus offering nutritional advantages for those on cholesterol lowering diets. Fatty fish, in particular, such as salmon, swordfish, arctic char and sardines, are high in omega three fatty acids, which are known anti-inflammatory agents. Omega three fatty acids are also known to help with mood, attention and focus, decreasing allergic symptoms and joint pain associated with rheumatoid arthritis. Look for cold water fish when choosing a fatty fish for omega content. Lean white fish are generally good choices for those who have difficulty digesting fatty foods.

Crisp Lemony Baked Fish

Serves 4

1½ cups corn flakes or Mesa Sunrise cereal, crushed
¼ cup parmesan cheese, shredded
1 tablespoon ground flax seed
2 tablespoons green onion tops only, minced
⅛ teaspoon ground black pepper
1 lemon
1 egg, beaten
4 small fillets haddock (3 ounces/each)

Directions:

1. Preheat oven to 400°F. Line baking sheet with parchment paper; set aside.
2. Combine cereal, cheese, green onion, and pepper on plate or shallow dish. Grate lemon peel and stir into mixture; reserve lemon.
3. Place beaten egg in a second shallow dish. Dip each fillet one at a time into the egg, then the cereal mixture, coating well on both sides.
4. Place coated fillets on prepared baking sheet. Spray top of fillets with cooking spray and bake about 10 minutes or until cooked through and fish flakes easily with a fork.
5. Cut reserved lemon into wedges and add as a garnish on serving plates.

Nutrient Analysis: cal 123/pro 21/carb 4/fiber 2/fat 3/sodium 147

Exchanges: 3 meat, 1 fat

Make it a Meal: 1 cup steamed zucchini, 1 small baked potato, and 1 tablespoon whipped butter with ground black pepper to taste.

Adapted from Diabetic Cooking

Lemon Rosemary Shrimp

and Vegetable Souvlaki

Serves 4

Skewer Ingredients
1 pound shrimp, peeled, deveined
1 large zucchini w/skin, halved lengthwise, sliced
1 large red bell pepper, cubed
8 green onions, trimmed
Sauce Ingredients
1 teaspoon lemon zest, grated
2 tablespoons lemon juice
1 tablespoon olive oil
2 cloves garlic, minced
⅛ teaspoon red pepper flakes
½ teaspoon fresh rosemary
Cooking spray

Directions:

1. Coat 4 (12-inch) bamboo or metal skewers with cooking spray.
2. Alternate threading shrimp, zucchini, bell pepper, and onions.
3. In a small bowl, stir together sauce ingredients and set aside.
4. Preheat grill to high heat. Coat grill rack or grill pan with cooking spray. Coat skewered ingredients with cooking spray.
5. Cook skewers 2 minutes on each side. Remove from heat, place on serving platter and spoon sauce evenly over all.

Nutrient Analysis: cal 184/pro 25/carb 9/fiber 3/fat 6/sodium 182

Exchanges: 3½ meat, ½ bread, 1 fat

Make it a Meal: Serve with ⅓ cup *Pan Roasted Quinoa* and 1 cup steamed sugar snap peas.

Adapted from Diabetic Cooking

Southern Crab Cakes

with Rémoulade Dipping Sauce

Serves 4

10 ounces fresh lump crabmeat
2 slices sourdough bread crumbs, divided
4 tablespoons ground flax seed
¼ cup green onion, chopped
¼ cup non-fat mayonnaise, divided
2 egg whites, lightly beaten
1 tablespoon spicy brown mustard, divided
½ teaspoon hot pepper sauce, divided
1 teaspoon olive oil
1 lemon, cut into wedges

Directions:

1. Preheat oven to 200°F.
2. Pick out and discard any shell or cartilage from crabmeat.
3. In a medium bowl, combine crabmeat, half bread crumbs, ground flax, green onions, 2 tablespoons mayonnaise, egg whites, ½ table-spoon mustard and ⅛ teaspoon hot pepper sauce; mix well.
4. Using ¼ of the mixture per cake, shape into 4½-inch-thick cakes. Roll each cake lightly in remaining bread crumbs.
5. Heat 1 teaspoon of oil in large skillet over medium-high heat.
6. Add crab cakes; cook 4 to 5 minutes per side or until golden brown.
7. Transfer to serving platter; keep warm in oven.
8. For the dipping sauce, combine remaining mayonnaise, mustard and hot sauce in a small bowl; mix well.
9. Serve crab cakes warm with dipping sauce and lemon wedges.

Nutrient Analysis: cal 210/pro 20/carb 17/fiber 3/fat 8/sodium 560

Exchanges: 3 meat, 1 bread, 1½ fat

Make it a Meal: Serve each crab cake with 1 cup steamed green beans and a small baked sweet potato.

Adapted from Diabetic Cooking

Fish Amandine

Serves 4

1 egg, beaten
¼ cup 1% milk
¼ cup flour
2 teaspoons lemon peel, grated
¼ teaspoon paprika
4 (4 ounce fillets) haddock, flounder, cod or scrod
Cooking spray
1 teaspoon butter or margarine, no added salt
¼ cup sliced almonds
½ cup green onion, sliced
3 tablespoons fresh lemon juice
4 sprigs fresh parsley, chopped

Directions:

1. In a shallow plate, combine egg and milk. In a second shallow plate, combine flour, lemon peel and paprika.
2. Coat each fish fillet one at a time in egg mixture, then coat evenly with flour mixture. Place on plate lined with wax paper.
3. Cover and chill at least 15 minutes.
4. Heat large, non-stick skillet over medium heat and add cooking spray. Add fillets and cook about 4 minutes on each side until golden brown, crisp and fish flakes with a fork. Remove fish and keep warm.
5. Wipe out skillet and add cooking spray and butter. Add sliced almonds to skillet and cook until golden brown, stirring often. Stir in green onion and lemon juice. Heat, stirring.
6. Serve sauce over fillets and sprinkle with parsley.

Nutrient Analysis: cal 213/pro 25/carb 14/fiber 1/fat 6/sodium 103

Exchanges: 4 meat, 1 bread, 1 fat

Make it a Meal: Serve with 1 cup steamed green beans & 1 serving (½ cup) of *Herbed Grains*.

Adapted from Try-Foods Intl., Inc., Apopka, FL

Linguine with White Clam Sauce

Serves 4

4 ounces linguine pasta
3 cloves garlic, minced
1 tablespoon olive oil
3 cans clams & juice from 2 cans
1 teaspoon chicken bouillon, lower sodium
1½ tablespoons flour
4 sprigs fresh parsley
1 dash ground black pepper
¼ cup white wine

Directions:

1. Prepare linguine according to directions on package.
2. Meanwhile, over medium heat sauté garlic in oil but do not allow to brown. Add clam juice, chicken bouillon; slowly add flour while stirring.
3. Add clams, parsley and pepper. Cook until mixture starts to bubble then remove from heat and add wine.
4. Toss with cooked linguine.

Nutrient Analysis: cal 252/pro 21/carb 27/fiber 3/fat 6/sodium 340

Exchanges: 3 meat, 1½ bread, 1 fat

Make it a Meal: Serve with a *Simple Side Salad* topped with white wine vinaigrette.

Tangy Topped Salmon

Serves 6

½ cup plain, fat-free Greek yogurt
½ cup skim milk
1 large egg, separated
1 large egg white
2 slices wheat bread, cubed
1 teaspoon garlic powder
1 teaspoon dried oregano
1 teaspoon ground cayenne pepper
1 pound salmon
¼ cup scallions
¼ cup celery
1 tablespoon lemon juice
¼ cup non-fat mayonnaise
1 tablespoon yellow mustard
1 tablespoon fresh parsley

Directions:

1. Preheat oven to 375° and grease casserole dish.
2. Combine yogurt, milk and egg yolk on medium speed in mixer.
3. Next mix in bread cubes and spices; let stand 5 minutes and beat smooth.
4. Add salmon, scallions, celery, and lemon juice into mixer. Mix and blend until well mashed.
5. Pour into a greased casserole dish and bake for 25–30 minutes.
6. While baking, mix mayonnaise and mustard.
7. Separately, beat egg whites until stiff and gently fold into mayonnaise mixture, creating a meringue.
8. Remove salmon from oven and top with meringue.
9. Bake for 5 additional minutes.
10. Sprinkle with parsley and serve.

Nutrient Analysis: cal 222/pro 21/carb 12/fiber 1/fat 10/sodium 270

Exchanges: 3 meat, 1 bread, 2 fat

Make it a Meal: Serve with steamed cauliflower & broccoli (½ cup each) + 1 large carrot, sliced & steamed.

Fish with Tomato Ragout on Shredded Sweet Potatoes

Serves 4

2 tablespoons flour
¼ teaspoon red pepper flakes
2 tablespoons unsalted butter, divided
4 fillets (about 1 pound) cod fillets or any white fish
6 cups water
3 sweet potatoes, peeled, shredded in food processor
1 dash ground black pepper
2 cloves garlic, minced
½ cup red onion, diced
2 cups plum tomatoes, diced
¼ cup fresh parsley, finely chopped
2 tablespoons capers, rinsed, drained

Directions:

1. Combine flour and red pepper flakes in a shallow dish and coat fillets with mixture.
2. Melt 1 tablespoon butter in a large, non-stick skillet over medium-high heat.
3. Place fillets in skillet; cook 4 to 6 minutes, carefully turning once, until fish flakes easily with fork. Remove from skillet and keep warm.
4. Meanwhile, bring 6 cups water to a boil in a large saucepan. Add shredded sweet potatoes and simmer until just tender, about 5 minutes. Drain and add ground pepper.
5. Heat butter in same skillet over medium-high heat. Add garlic and red onion; cook and stir 30 seconds.
6. Add tomato, parsley and capers; heat through.
7. Divide shredded potatoes among 4 plates; place fish fillet on potatoes; top with tomato ragout.

Nutrient Analysis: cal 278/pro 23/carb 31/fiber 5/fat 7/sodium 251

Exchanges: 3 meat, 2 bread, 1 fat

Make it a Meal: For each serving add 1 cup steamed Italian pole beans.

Adapted from Diabetic Cooking

Salmon Patties with Zesty

Honey-Mustard Sauce

Serves 6

Patty ingredients

½ cup onion, chopped

16 ounce can salmon

⅔ cup bread crumbs, divided

½ cup egg substitute

1 tablespoon butter substitute granules

1 tablespoon water

½ cup fresh parsley

1 teaspoon dry/ground mustard

Cooking spray

Sauce Ingredients

1 cup non-fat plain yogurt

1 tablespoon honey

1 tablespoon spicy brown mustard

Directions:

1. Drain salmon.
2. Heat a large, non-stick skillet over medium heat and coat with cooking spray; sauté onion.
3. In a bowl, mix salmon, sautéed onion, ½ cup bread crumbs, egg substitute, butter substitute, water and spices.
4. Put remaining bread crumbs in shallow dish. Form 6 patties out of salmon mixture then coat each patty in bread crumbs on both sides.
5. Coat skillet with cooking spray again and sauté patties until browned on both sides (approx. 5-6 minutes total).
6. For the sauce, mix all ingredients and serve with patties.

Nutrient Analysis: cal 183/pro 20/carb 12/fiber 0/fat 6/sodium 236

Exchanges: 3 meat, 1 bread, 1 fat

Make it a Meal: Add 1 cup steamed broccoli and 1 serving *Sautéed Grains* per plate OR

Serve on a whole wheat mini pita with a *Simple Side Salad.*

Vegetarian

Vegetarian entrees are very popular for a variety of reasons: personal preference for animal rights, health qualities, digestive issues that may arise with flesh proteins in some individuals. In order for a vegetarian food to offer adequate protein, there needs to be an adequate amount of essential amino acids supplied in the diet. While health professionals disagree about the need for complementing these amino acids at the meal, this cookbook does offer complete complementarity within the "Make It A Meal" suggestions. The amount of protein supplied at each meal will also be very close to that of a meat, fish, pork or poultry entrée, ensuring adequate intake. A few distinct advantages to most vegetarian selections are that they are a good source of dietary fiber and are low in saturated fat. The selections here vary from soy based to other legume and grain based entrees.

Almond Rice Loaf

Serves 10

3 cups cubed bread
¼ cup rolled oats
1 cup milk, 1%
2 cups brown rice, cooked
3 tablespoons natural, creamy peanut butter, no added salt
2 cups almonds, chopped
1 tablespoon soy sauce, lower sodium
¼ cup onion, chopped
2 tablespoons fresh parsley, chopped

Directions:

1. Preheat oven to 350°F.
2. Soak bread and oats in milk.
3. Blend the rice, peanut butter, and almonds with a fork.
4. Add to bread mixture and mix well with the rest of the ingredients.
5. Bake in a square baking dish or small loaf pan for 35 minutes.

Nutrient Analysis: cal 231/pro 8/carb 22/fiber 4/fat 13/sodium 85

Exchanges: 1 meat, 1 bread, 2½ fat

Make it a Meal: 2 cups fresh, steamed vegetables, ¼ cup sweet potatoes.

Edamame-Chickpea Stew

Serves 8

2 cups chickpeas (garbanzo beans)
2 cups frozen, shelled edamame (soybeans)
Cooking spray
1 cup red onion, chopped
3 cloves garlic, minced
1 - 14½ ounce can diced tomatoes, no added salt
¼ cup lemon juice
1 tablespoon fresh parsley, chopped
1 tablespoon fresh mint, chopped
1 dash kosher salt
½ teaspoon ground cumin
⅛ teaspoon ground red pepper
⅛ teaspoon ground cinnamon
1 dash ground cloves

Directions:

1. Place chickpeas in a large saucepan; cover with water to 2 inches above chickpeas. Bring to boil; cover, reduce heat and simmer 40 minutes or until tender. Drain well and set aside.
2. Place edamame in a small saucepan; cover with water to 2 inches above edamame. Bring to boil; cook 2 minutes or until edamame are tender. Drain well and set aside.
3. In Dutch oven over medium-high heat coat with cooking spray. Add onion, garlic, and tomatoes. Sauté 6 minutes or until onion is translucent, stirring often.
4. Stir in lentils, edamame and remaining ingredients. Cook 2 minutes or until thoroughly heated.

Nutrient Analysis: cal 225/pro 13/carb 35/fiber 10/fat 4/sodium 28

Exchanges: 2 meat, 1½ bread, 1 fat

Make it a Meal: *Simple Side Salad* and ½ ounce of shredded mozzarella either over stew or over salad.

Adapted from Cooking Light Magazine, December 2008

Hominy-Pinto Burgers with

Roasted Poblano Chiles

Serves 4

1 poblano chile pepper
Cooking spray
2 tablespoons onion, chopped
2 cloves garlic, minced
1- 15½ ounce can pinto beans, rinsed, drained
½ of a 15 ounce can hominy, rinsed, drained
1½ tablespoons ground flaxseed
2 tablespoons cornmeal
1 cup Monterey Jack cheese w/ jalapeno peppers, shredded
6 tablespoons plain Greek yogurt, fat-free
3 tablespoons salsa, low-sodium

Directions:

1. Preheat broiler. Place chile on a foil-lined baking sheet; broil 3 inches from heat for 8 minutes until blackened and charred, turning after 6 minutes.
2. Place chile in a heavy-duty plastic bag and seal. Let stand 15 minutes.
3. Peel and discard skin. Cut the chile lengthwise into 4 strips; discard seeds. Set aside.
4. Heat large non-stick skillet over medium heat and coat with cooking spray.
5. Add onion and garlic; sauté 5 minutes. Place onion mixture, beans and hominy in a food processor; pulse until coarsely ground.
6. In a medium bowl, combine bean mixture and ground flax seed.
7. Divide mixture into 4 equal portions and shape each into a ½-inch-thick patty.

144

8. Place cornmeal in a shallow dish and coat each patty with the cornmeal.
9. Heat skillet over medium heat and lightly coat with cooking spray. Add patties and cook 4 minutes. Turn patties over and top each with 2 tablespoons of cheese. Cook additional 4 minutes.
10. In a small bowl, combine plain yogurt and salsa.
11. Top each patty with 1 heaping tablespoon of salsa mixture and a pepper strip.

Nutrient Analysis: cal 285/prot 15/carb 32/fiber 8/fat 10/sodium 764

Exchanges: 2 meat, 2 bread, 2 fat

Make it a Meal: For an easy side, mix ¼ cup chopped red bell pepper, ¼ cup cooked pinto beans, 1 tablespoons chopped red onion, 2 teaspoons chopped fresh cilantro, 2 teaspoons fresh lime juice.

Adapted from Cooking Light Magazine

Lentils and Rice

Serves 6

2⅔ cups chicken broth, fat-free, less sodium
¾ cup dry lentils
½ cup onion, chopped
½ cup dry brown rice
¼ cup white wine
½ teaspoon dried basil
¼ teaspoon dried oregano
¼ teaspoon dried thyme
⅛ teaspoon garlic powder
⅛ teaspoon ground black pepper
4 ounces Swiss cheese, reduced fat
Cooking spray

Directions:

1. Preheat oven to 350°F.
2. In a large bowl combine chicken broth, lentils, onion, uncooked rice, wine and seasonings. Shred half of the cheese and stir into lentil mixture.
3. Coat a 1½ quart baking dish with cooking spray and pour lentil mixture into the dish.
4. Bake, covered, for 1½ to 2 hours until lentils and rice are done, stirring twice.
5. Shred remaining cheese on top and bake 2 to 3 minutes longer.

Nutrient Analysis: cal 219/pro 13/carb 30/fiber 9/fat 5/sodium 279

Exchanges: 2 meat, 1 1/2 bread, 1 fat

Make it a Meal: Serve with a *Simple Side Salad*, 1/2 toasted millet lavash or mini wheat pita

Swiss Pie

Serves 6

1 tablespoon light margarine or light butter
26 Triscuit wheat crackers, reduced-fat, crushed
Cooking spray
½ cup onion, chopped
2 medium eggs
¾ cup plain Greek yogurt, fat-free
2 tablespoons ground flax seed
1 dash ground black pepper
8 ounces Swiss cheese, low-fat, shredded
2 ounces cheddar cheese, reduced-fat, shredded
1 tablespoon fresh parsley, chopped

Directions:

1. Preheat oven to 375°F.
2. Melt margarine/butter and combine with crushed crackers. Spray with cooking spray to coat additional crumbs; mix well. Press into 8-inch pie plate.
3. In a small skillet coated with cooking spray, sauté chopped onion.
4. In a bowl, combine onion, eggs, yogurt, flax, pepper and Swiss; pour into pie shell.
5. Sprinkle with cheddar and parsley and bake for 25-30 minutes. Let set 5 minutes before serving.

Nutrient Analysis: cal 248/pro 20/carb 20/fiber 3/fat 9/sodium 340

Exchanges: 3 meat, 1 bread, 2 fat

Make it a Meal: Serve with oven-roasted asparagus (1 teaspoon olive oil, kosher salt; roast at 400°F for about 10 minutes) and ½ cup steamed carrots.

Wheat Berry Salad with Fava Beans

Serves 6

½ cup wheat berries (or gluten-free alternative like quinoa)
4 cups water
2½ cups fava beans, shelled
½ cup sun dried tomatoes packed in oil, drained
½ cup celery, chopped
2 tablespoons dried currants
3 tablespoons balsamic vinegar
1 teaspoon olive oil
½ teaspoon ground black pepper
2 cloves garlic, crushed
¼ cup fresh parsley, chopped
6 outer leaves romaine lettuce

Directions:

1. Place wheat berries in large saucepan; cover with water 2 inches above wheat berries. Bring to boil. Cover, reduce heat, and simmer 1½ hours or until wheat berries are tender. Drain.
2. In a medium saucepan bring 4 cups of water to a boil. Add shelled fava beans; cook 2 minutes. Drain and rinse with cold water; drain. Remove and discard tough outer skins from beans.
3. In a large bowl combine wheat berries, fava beans, tomatoes, celery and currants.
4. In a small bowl, combine vinegar, oil, ground pepper and garlic, stirring with a whisk. Drizzle over wheat berry mixture; toss well to coat.
5. Arrange lettuce leaf on each plate and spoon equal amount onto each leaf. Sprinkle with parsley and serve.

Nutrient Analysis: cal 180/pro 8/carb 32/fiber 8/fat 3/sodium 246

Exchanges: 1 meat, 1½ bread, 1 fat

Make it a Meal: Top with 1½ ounces crumbled goat cheese and serve ½ piece of toasted millet and flax lavash on the side.

Adapted from Cooking Light Magazine

Baked Falafel Sandwiches

with Yogurt-Tahini Sauce

Serves 6

Sauce Ingredients:
1 cup plain Greek yogurt, fat-free
1 tablespoon tahini (sesame butter)
1 tablespoon lemon juice
Falafel Ingredients:
¾ cup water
¼ cup bulgur (or quinoa), uncooked
2 cups chickpeas (garbanzo beans), cooked
½ cup fresh cilantro, chopped
½ cup green onion, chopped
½ cup sweet green pepper, chopped
½ cup cucumber, peeled, pared, chopped
⅓ cup water
2 tablespoons all-purpose flour
1 tablespoon ground cumin
1 teaspoon baking powder, low salt
3 cloves garlic
1 dash kosher salt
Cooking spray
Sandwich Ingredients:
6 mini pita breads, 100% whole wheat
12 thin-slices tomato

Directions:

1. To prepare sauce, combine first three ingredients, stirring with a whisk until blended. Cover and chill until ready to serve.

2. Bring ¾ cup water to a boil in a small saucepan; add bulgur (or quinoa) to pan. Remove from heat; cover and let stand 30 minutes or until tender. Drain and set aside.
3. Preheat oven to 425°F.
4. In a food processor combine chickpeas, cilantro, onion, pepper, cucumber, water, flour, cumin, baking powder, garlic and salt; pulse 10 times or until well blended and smooth (mixture will be wet).
5. Spoon chickpea mixture into a large bowl and stir in bulgur (or quinoa).
6. Divide mixture into 12 equal portions (about ¼ cup) and shape each into a ¼-inch patty.
7. Place patties on a baking sheet coated with cooking spray. Bake for 10 minutes on each side until browned.
8. Spread about 2½ tablespoons of sauce into each pita. Insert each with 2 falafel patties and 2 tomato slices.

Nutrient Analysis: cal 248/pro 13/carb 41/fiber 9/fat 4/ sodium 235

Exchanges: 2 meat, 2 bread, 1 fat

Make It A Meal: serve with a *Simple Salad*

Adapted from Cooking Light Magazine, December 2007

Eggless Tofu "Egg" Salad Sandwich

Serves 6

1 block tofu, extra firm, ideally organic
¼ cup light mayonnaise
1 tablespoon mustard
1 tablespoon soy sauce, lower sodium, wheat-free
2 tablespoons parsley, chopped
¼ teaspoon garlic powder
6 mini pita breads, 100% whole wheat

Directions:

1. Combine tofu, mayonnaise, mustard, soy sauce, parsley and garlic powder in a food processor/blender or mix with fork.
2. Serve in pita with lettuce, if desired.

Nutrient Analysis: cal 199/pro 13/carb 17/fiber 3/fat 9/sodium 383

Exchanges: 2 meat, 1 bread, 2 fat

Make it a Meal: *Simple Side Salad,* ½ serving healthy chips such as "Food Should Taste Good" or "Terra".

Lentil Burgers

Serves 4

Burger Ingredients:
14½ ounce can chicken broth, non-fat, lower sodium
1 cup lentils
1 small carrot
¼ cup mushrooms
1 medium egg
¼ cup bread crumbs
3 tablespoons onion, chopped
2 cloves garlic
1 teaspoon dried, ground thyme
Cooking spray
4 leafs romaine lettuce
Sauce Ingredients:
¼ cup plain Greek yogurt, fat-free
¼ cup cucumber, peeled, chopped
¼ teaspoon dried dill weed
¼ teaspoon ground black pepper
½ teaspoon dried spearmint leaf
⅛ teaspoon hot pepper sauce

Directions:

1. Over high heat bring chicken broth to a boil in a medium saucepan.
2. Stir in lentils, reduce heat to low, simmer covered about 30 minutes or until lentils are tender and liquid is absorbed. Let cool to room temperature.
3. Place lentils, carrot and mushrooms in food processor or blender; process until finely chopped but not fully smooth.
4. Transfer lentil mixture to a bowl; stir in egg, breadcrumbs, onion, garlic and thyme. Refrigerate, covered, 2 to 3 hours.
5. Shape lentil mixture into 4 (½-inch-thick) patties.

6. Coat large, non-stick skillet with cooking spray; heat over medium heat. Cook patties over medium-low heat for about 10 minutes or until browned on each side.
7. 7.For sauce, combine remaining ingredients in a bowl.
8. 8.Arrange a lettuce leaf on each plate. Place a burger on each leaf and serve sauce over burgers.

Nutrient Analysis: cal 231/pro 17/carb 35/fiber 16/fat 3/sodium 112

Exchanges: 2 meat, 1 bread, 1 fat

Make it a Meal: Serve on ½ Millet & Flax Lavash (flatbread) with a side of baby carrots.

Adapted from Diabetic Cooking

Oatmeal Walnut Patties

Serves 4

½ cup egg substitute
¾ cup quick rolled oats
¼ cup walnuts, chopped
¼ cup non-fat milk
1 small onion, raw
¼ teaspoon ground sage
2 teaspoons soy sauce, lower sodium, wheat-free
Cooking spray
4 mini pita breads, 100% whole wheat
4 inner-leafs green leaf lettuce
4 slices tomato

Directions:

1. Beat eggs. Add all ingredients to bowl and let set for 5 minutes.
2. Divide into 4 equal portions and form each into a patty.
3. Heat a large, non-stick skillet over medium-high heat and coat with cooking spray.
4. Add patties to pan and cook for 3 minutes on each side or until browned.
5. Assemble each sandwich by placing one cooked patty, piece of lettuce and slice of tomato into each pita.

Nutrient Analysis: cal 221/pro 12/carb 28/fiber 5/fat 8/sodium 332

Exchanges: 2 meat, 1½ bread, 1½ fat

Make it a Meal: 1 serving of *Waldorf Salad* with 2 tablespoons shredded low-fat cheddar cheese sprinkled on top.

Tofu Steaks with Red Pepper-Walnut Sauce

Serves 6

14 ounces extra-firm, water-packed tofu, reduced-fat, organic
¼ cup fresh basil, chopped
¼ cup water
2 tablespoons fresh parsley, chopped
1 tablespoon fresh thyme, chopped
2 tablespoons white wine vinegar
1 tablespoon Dijon mustard
1 dash kosher salt
½ teaspoon crushed red pepper
8 cloves garlic, minced
½ cup all-purpose flour
½ cup egg substitute
2 cups Panko bread crumbs (Japanese-style bread crumbs)
1 tablespoon olive oil
3 tablespoons toasted walnuts, chopped
1 - 12 ounce bottle roasted red peppers, drained

Directions:

1. Cut tofu crosswise into 4 slices. Place tofu slices on several layers of heavy-duty paper towels; cover with additional paper towels. Let stand 30 minutes, pressing down occasionally.
2. In a large zip-top bag, combine basil, water, parsley, thyme, wine vinegar, Dijon mustard, salt, crushed red pepper and garlic.
3. Add tofu to bag and seal. Marinate in refrigerator 1 hour, turning bag occasionally.
4. Place flour in a shallow dish. Place egg substitute in another shallow dish. Place Panko in a third shallow dish.
5. Remove tofu from marinade, reserving remaining marinade.
6. Working with one piece of tofu at a time, dredge tofu in flour, shaking off excess. Dip tofu in egg substitute, allowing excess to drip off.

Then coat tofu completely with Panko, pressing slightly to adhere. Set aside.

7. Repeat coating procedure with remaining tofu, flour, egg substitute and Panko.
8. Heat a large, non-stick skillet over medium-high heat. Add olive oil to pan, swirling to coat.
9. Add tofu to pan, reduce to medium heat and cook for 4 minutes on each side or until browned. Remove tofu from pan and keep warm.
10. Combine reserved marinade, walnuts, and bell peppers in a blender; process until smooth, about 2 minutes.
11. Pour bell pepper mixture into pan; cook over medium-high heat 2 minutes or until thoroughly heated. Serve with tofu.

Nutrient Analysis: cal 219/pro 12/carb 29/fiber 2/fat 6/sodium 356

Exchanges: 2 meat, 2 bread,1 fat

Make it a Meal: 1 cup steamed zucchini and ½ serving *Herbed Grains* w/1 teaspoon ground flax.

Adapted from Cooking Light Magazine, December 2008

Black Bean Cakes with Salsa Cruda

Serves 6

Salsa Cruda Ingredients:

1 cup tomato, chopped, seeded

2 tablespoons onion, minced

2 tablespoons fresh cilantro, chopped

2 tablespoons lime juice

½ jalapeno pepper, seeded, minced

1 clove garlic, minced

Bean Cake Ingredients:

2 - 15 ounce cans black beans, lower sodium, rinsed, drained

¼ cup all-purpose flour, (or gluten-free alternative)

¼ cup fresh cilantro, chopped

¼ cup plain Greek yogurt, fat-free

1 medium egg

1 tablespoon canola oil

1 tablespoon chili powder

2 cloves garlic, minced

Cooking spray

6 mini pita breads, 100% whole wheat

Directions:

1. To prepare salsa, combine all salsa ingredients in a small bowl and refrigerate for at least 1 hour before serving.
2. For cakes, place beans in a medium bowl; mash with fork or potato masher until almost smooth, leaving some beans in larger pieces.
3. Stir in flour, cilantro, yogurt, egg, oil, chili powder and garlic.
4. Heat a large, non-stick skillet over medium-high and coat with cooking spray.
5. For each cake, drop 2 heaping tablespoonfuls of bean mixture onto skillet; flatten to form cake.

6. Cook 6 to 8 minutes or until lightly browned, turning once. Serve on pita with Salsa Cruda.

Nutrient Analysis: cal 217/pro 12/carb 39/fiber 10/fat 4/sodium 456

Exchanges: 2 meat, 2 bread, 1 fat

Make it a Meal: Side of greens: 1 cup spinach, ¾ cup green lettuce, and ¼ cup radicchio and corn (1 ear or ½ cup) tossed with 1 teaspoon olive oil and 2 teaspoons lime juice, ½ ounce shredded low-fat monterey jack cheese sprinkled on top.

Adapted from Diabetic Cooking

Falafel Burger

Serves 8

Sauce Ingredients:

¼ cup tahini (sesame paste)

1 cup hot water

3 tablespoons lemon juice

2 cloves garlic, minced

2 tablespoons plain whey protein powder

Patty Ingredients:

1 cup red onion, chopped

½ cup fresh parsley, chopped

2 tablespoons lemon juice

1 teaspoon ground cumin

1 teaspoon ground coriander

2 – 15.5 ounce cans chickpeas (garbanzo), rinsed, drained

4 cloves garlic, minced

½ cup bread crumbs, divided

Cooking spray

Additional Ingredients:

8 outer-leafs romaine lettuce

2 cups tomato, chopped

2 cups cucumber, peeled, chopped

½ cup red onion, chopped

4 ounces feta, reduced fat, crumbled

Directions:

1. To prepare sauce, place first 4 ingredients in a blender and process until smooth.
2. For the burger patties, combine onion, parsley, lemon juice, cumin, coriander, chickpeas and garlic in food processor. Process until smooth, scraping sides of bowl occasionally.
3. Place bean mixture in a large bowl; stir in ¼ cup breadcrumbs.

4. Divide bean mixture into 8 equal portions, shaping each into a ½-inch-thick patty.
5. Place remaining breadcrumbs into a shallow dish and coat patties with breadcrumbs.
6. Heat a large, non-stick skillet over medium-high and coat with cooking spray.
7. Add 4 patties to pan and cook for 3 minutes on each side or until browned. Repeat procedure for remaining patties.
8. Place a romaine lettuce leaf on each serving plate. In a bowl, mix the chopped tomato, cucumber, and onion. Divide the tomato mixture into six portions and arrange on each lettuce leaf. Place cooked patty on top of tomato mixture and drizzle each serving with about 3 tablespoons of sauce.

Nutrient Analysis: cal 260/pro 14/carb 36/fiber 8/fat 7/sodium 549

Exchanges: 2 meat, 2 bread, 1½ fat

Make it a meal: 1 serving *Pita Crisps* or ½ millet flax lavash, toasted. Optional - top with 1 tablespoon chia seeds for additional 2 grams protein.

Adapted from Cooking Light Magazine

Lentil Loaf

Serves 8 (2 "muffins" each)

1 cup lentils, dry
2 cups boiling water
1 medium onion, chopped
¼ teaspoon garlic powder
1 cup wheat germ
⅔ cup whole wheat bread crumbs
1 teaspoon ground oregano
1 teaspoon ground sage
½ teaspoon dried basil
½ teaspoon dried thyme
¼ teaspoon ground black pepper
3 tablespoons olive oil
1 cup evaporated skim milk
2 tablespoons walnuts, chopped
8 ounces tomato sauce, no added salt

Directions:

1. Drop lentils into boiling water. Cook on low for 1 hour.
2. Preheat oven to 350°F.
3. Heat a small skillet over medium and lightly coat with cooking spray; sauté onion until translucent.
4. After lentils are cooked, mash until lumpy; spoon into a bowl.
5. Add onion and remaining ingredients except tomato sauce into bowl; mix.
6. Coat 9 x 4 loaf pan or 16 muffin tins with cooking spray; place mixture into pan. Bake for 1 hour.
7. Pour tomato sauce over loaf or "muffins" and bake an additional 20 minutes. Remove from oven and let set 15 minutes before slicing.

Nutrient Analysis: cal 229/pro 12/carb 31/fiber 10/fat 7/sodium 64

Exchanges: 2 meat, 1 1/2 bread, 1 1/2 fat

Make it a Meal: Serve with ½ cup baked acorn squash and ⅓ cup cooked, shelled edamame.

Red Lentils and Bulgur Bake

Serves 8

1½ cups red lentils, rinsed
2 cups water
1 dash kosher salt
¼ teaspoon ground black pepper
1 bay leaf
1 teaspoon dried oregano
1 teaspoon dried basil
½ teaspoon dried thyme
½ teaspoon dried marjoram
1 large onion, chopped
4 cloves garlic, minced
1 - 28 ounce can diced tomatoes, no added salt
¾ cup bulgur wheat or quinoa
2 medium carrots, chopped
1 cup celery, chopped
1 medium green bell pepper, chopped
1½ cups mozzarella cheese, part-skim, shredded
¼ cup fresh parsley, chopped

Directions:

1. Preheat oven to 350°F and coat 9 X 15-inch baking dish with cooking spray.
2. In a large saucepan, combine lentils, water, salt, pepper, bay leaf, herbs, onion, garlic and tomatoes. Bring to boil and simmer 30 minutes.
3. Remove from heat. Add bulgur and vegetables; mix well.
4. Pour mixture into dish; cover and bake for 35 minutes.
5. Combine cheese and parsley and sprinkle on top; bake uncovered for an additional 5 minutes.

Nutrient Analysis: cal 252/pro 17/carb 35/fiber 9/fat 5/sodium 163

Exchanges: 2 meat, 2 bread, 1 fat

Make it a Meal: *Garlicky Mustard Greens* (1/2 serving).

Veggie "Meatballs"

Serves 6

½ cup water
¾ cup quinoa
Cooking spray
3 medium Portobello mushrooms, stemmed, diced
2 tablespoons onion, chopped
½ small zucchini, coarsely grated
1 teaspoon dried Italian seasoning
2 cloves garlic, minced
¼ cup sun dried tomatoes, chopped (not packed in oil)
4 ounces grated parmesan cheese, reduced-fat
2 large egg whites
1 large egg, whole
2 tablespoons ground flaxseed

Directions:

1. Preheat oven to 375°F.
2. Bring water to a boil in small saucepan. Remove from heat, add quinoa, cover and let stand while preparing vegetables.
3. Heat a large, non-stick skillet over medium-high and coat with cooking spray.
4. Add mushrooms, onion, zucchini and Italian seasoning. Cook and stir until softened, about 8 minutes.
5. Add garlic; cook 1 minute while stirring constantly. Stir in tomatoes.
6. Transfer mixture to large bowl and let stand to cool slightly. Add quinoa, cheese and eggs. Stir to mix well.
7. Cover large rimmed baking pan with cooking spray.
8. Shape mixture into 12 balls, using approximately ¼ cup mixture for each.
9. Place in pan and bake for 20 minutes. Turn meatballs over and bake additional 8 to 10 minutes or until browned.

Nutrient Analysis: cal 200/pro 10/carb 26/fiber 3/fat 7/sodium 367

Exchanges: 1½ meat, 1½ bread, 1 fat

Make it a Meal: ½ ounce dry pasta cooked, ¼ cup pasta sauce, ¾ cup peas.

Adapted from Diabetic Cooking

Grains and Starches

Grains and starches provide a good source of carbohydrate energy, or as I like to call it, the gas to the car engine! Grains offer bulk and fullness to a meal, and some provide magnesium which keeps blood pressure normal, helps with sleep and stress and also plays a role in proper digestion. Sweet potatoes and butternut squash are excellent sources of fiber, vitamin B6, beta-carotene, the vibrant orange color seen in other deep yellow-orange fruits and vegetables. Many popular diets de-emphasize the importance of grain foods, often blaming "carbs" for the obesity epidemic in this country. The starch and grain options provided here are in a quantity that provides adequate fuel, fiber and vitamins and minerals – not even closely resembling the puffy bagels and breads commonly eaten.

Baked Sweet Potatoes with

Maple-Jalapeño Sour Cream

Serves 3

3 small sweet potatoes, scrubbed, dried
½ cup plain, fat-free Greek yogurt
½ teaspoon chili powder
1 tablespoon maple syrup
2 teaspoons jalapeno pepper, seeded, minced
1 teaspoon lime juice

Directions:

1. Preheat oven to 450° with rack positioned in the center.
2. Bake the clean, dry potatoes directly on rack for about 40 minutes, or until soft when pierced.
3. Combine all topping ingredients; chill until ready to serve.

Nutrient Analysis: cal 94/pro 5/carb 19/fiber 2/fat 0/sodium 41

Exchanges: 1 bread

Adapted from Cuisine At Home Magazine

Grilled Garlic Naan

Serves 4

1 clove garlic, minced
½ tablespoon ground flaxseeds
1 teaspoon chia seeds
1 teaspoon olive oil
4 ounces (about ½ package) Tandoori Naan, garlic

Directions:

1. Preheat oven to 400° F.
2. Mix the minced garlic, flax, chia, and olive oil together in a small bowl.
3. Lightly brush the surface of the Naan breads with the flavored oil.
4. Bake Naan 2 to 3 minutes on each side.
5. Cut into large triangles and serve.

Nutrient Analysis: cal 91/pro 1.5/carb 13.5/fiber 1.5/fat 3/sodium 205.5

Exchanges: ½ bread

Mediterranean Orzo and Vegetable Pilaf

Serves 8

6 ounces orzo
Cooking spray
1 small onion, diced
2 cloves garlic, minced
1 large zucchini, diced
¾ cup chicken broth, non-fat, low-sodium
1 - 14 ounce can artichokes, drained, quartered
1 medium tomato, chopped
½ teaspoon dried oregano
¼ teaspoon ground black pepper
1 ounce feta cheese, reduced fat, crumbled
6 pitted black olives, sliced

Directions:

1. Cook orzo according to package instructions, omitting salt and fat. Drain; keep warm.
2. Heat a large, non-stick skillet over medium-high and lightly coat with cooking spray; sauté onion until tender, about 5 minutes. Add garlic; cook and stir 1 minute.
3. Add zucchini and chicken broth to skillet. Reduce heat; simmer about 5 minutes or until zucchini is crisp-tender.
4. Add cooked orzo, artichokes, tomato, oregano and ground pepper to skillet; cook and stir about 1 minute or until heated through.
5. Sprinkle each serving with feta cheese and top with black olives.

Nutrient Analysis: cal 115/pro 5.25/carb 22/fiber 3/fat 1.5/sodium 247

Exchanges: 1 bread, 1/2 vegetable

Adapted from Diabetic Cooking

Pan Roasted Quinoa

Serves 8

2 teaspoons olive oil
2 cups water
1 cup quinoa

Directions:

1. Heat olive oil in a large skillet over medium-high heat. Add the dry quinoa and sauté for 2 minutes, stirring as it browns.
2. Add 2 cups of water and bring to boil.
3. Reduce heat to simmer, cover and cook until water is absorbed.

Nutrient Analysis: cal 89/pro 3/carb 15/fiber 1.5/fat 2/sodium 15

Exchanges: ½ meat, 1 bread, 1 fat

Sautéed Grains

Serves 8

2 teaspoons olive oil
1 cup mixed grain:
    ⅓ cup long grain brown rice
    ⅓ cup millet
    ⅓ cup quinoa
2 cups vegetable cooking stock or water

Directions:

1. Heat oil in a pot. Sauté 1 cup of grains in oil until it smells like popcorn.
2. Add stock or water and cook until absorbed (approx. 25 minutes).

Nutrient Analysis: cal 104/pro 3/carb 18/fiber 1/fat 2/sodium 147

Exchanges: 1 bread

Butternut Squash Gratin with

Blue Cheese and Sage

Serves 5

3 cups butternut squash, cubed (¾ inch cubes)
1 slice bread
2 teaspoons olive oil
Cooking spray
1 cup onion, thinly sliced
1 teaspoon fresh sage, chopped
¼ teaspoon ground black pepper
¼ cup blue cheese, crumbled

Directions:

1. Preheat oven to 400°F.
2. Steam squash, covered for 10 minutes or until tender.
3. Place bread in a food processor and pulse 12 times or until coarse crumbs measure ½ cup. Transfer to small bowl; add 2 teaspoons oil and toss with a fork to combine. Set aside.
4. Heat a large, non-stick skillet over medium-high and coat with cooking spray. Add sliced onion to pan; sauté 5 minutes or until tender, stirring occasionally.
5. Transfer onion to a large bowl and add squash, sage and pepper to bowl. Toss gently.
6. Coat 11 x 7-inch baking dish with cooking spray; spoon in squash mixture.
7. Bake at 400°F for 20 minutes. Sprinkle crumbled blue cheese evenly over squash mixture, then sprinkle evenly with breadcrumb mixture.
8. Bake an additional 10 minutes until cheese is melted and crumbs are golden brown.

Nutrient Analysis: cal 102/pro 3/carb 15/fiber 2/fat 4/sodium 128

Exchanges: 1 bread, 1 fat

Adapted from Jackie Mills, MS, RD, Cooking Light Magazine, December 2008

Herbed Grains

Serves 6

2 tablespoons green onion, finely chopped
Cooking spray
1 cup water
⅓ cup long grain brown rice
⅓ cup quinoa
1 teaspoon or 1 cube chicken bouillon, low-sodium
1 teaspoon fresh basil, chopped
1 teaspoon fresh thyme, chopped
¼ teaspoon ground black pepper
½ cup fresh parsley, chopped
2 tablespoons chia seeds

Directions:

1. Heat a large, non-stick skillet and coat with cooking spray; sauté onion until tender.
2. Add water, rice and quinoa to skillet; cook 1 minute stirring.
3. Add bouillon, basil, thyme and pepper. Bring to boil; cover and reduce heat. Simmer 20 to 25 minutes or until liquid is absorbed.
4. Remove from heat and let cool 5 minutes. Stir in parsley and chia seeds.

Nutrient Analysis: cal 101/carb 17/fiber 3/fat 2/sodium 110

Exchanges: 1 bread

Pita Crisps

Serves 3

3 whole wheat, mini Pita breads
Cooking spray

Directions:

1. Preheat oven to 400°F. Coat baking sheet with cooking spray.
2. Split pitas horizontally so that you have two slices or sheets. Cut each of those into halves and then cut each half into quarters.
3. Arrange on baking sheet and spray tops with cooking spray. Bake until crisp.

Nutrient Analysis: cal 70/pro 3/carb 13/fiber 2/fat 1/sodium 150

Exchanges: 1 bread

Roasted Butternut Squash with Rosemary

Serves 6

3 cups butternut squash, cubed (¾ inch cubes)
2 shallots, diced
1 tablespoon olive oil
1 teaspoon fresh rosemary
½ teaspoon sugar
½ teaspoon ground black pepper
2 tablespoons ground flax seed

Directions:

1. Preheat oven to 450°F.
2. Toss squash cubes and shallots in plastic bag with oil to coat. Spread onto baking sheet; sprinkle with spices and ground flax.
3. Bake for 20 minutes. Turn and bake for 10 to 15 more minutes.

Nutrient Analysis: cal 85/pro 2/carb 14/fiber 2/fat 3/sodium 7

Exchanges: 1 bread, 1 fat

Savory Lentil Salad

Serves 12

1½ cups lentils
6 cups water
¼ teaspoon kosher salt
1 bay leaf
1 clove garlic, minced
1 tablespoon prepared Dijon mustard
1 tablespoon lemon juice
1 tablespoon wine vinegar
¼ teaspoon hot pepper sauce
½ cup onion, finely minced
3 tablespoons olive oil
1 medium green bell pepper, chopped
1 medium red bell pepper, chopped

Directions:

1. Bring lentils, water, salt and bay leaf to simmer. Cook, partially covered, for about 35 minutes. Drain lentils and return to pan. Remove bay leaf.
2. In a bowl, combine remaining ingredients and whisk in olive oil.
3. Fold sauce into lentils. Chill or serve warm.

Nutrient Analysis: cal 106/pro 6/carb 17/fiber 8/fat 1/sodium 114

Exchanges: 1 meat, ½ bread

Crispy Spiced Almond Wontons
***Serving Comment:Recipe makes 20 wont-
ons (5 servings = 4 wontons each)***

Serves 5

⅓ cup sliced almonds
1 teaspoon sugar
1 teaspoon ground flax seeds
1 teaspoon five-spice powder
Cooking spray
10 wonton-wrappers, 3.5" square
1 egg white, lightly beaten

Directions:

1. Preheat oven to 425°F.
2. Put almonds in a plastic bag and use a rolling pin or bottom of a heavy pan to crush the almonds coarsely.
3. Put the almonds in a bowl and mix with sugar, flax, and spice powder. Toss lightly to mix.
4. Lightly coat cookie sheet with cooking spray and arrange the wonton wrappers side by side on the pan.
5. Brush each with egg white and sprinkle almond mixture on top.
6. Using a sharp pizza cutter, cut the wontons from one corner to the opposite corner to create triangles.
7. Bake 5 minutes until golden brown and remove promptly from cookie sheet. Place on a cooling rack.
8. Once cool, transfer to serving dish.

Nutrient Analysis: cal 92/pro 4/carb 12/fiber 1/fat 4/sodium 103

Exchanges: 1 bread, 1 fat

Adapted from Nina Simonds, Whole Foods Market InSeason (2007)

Honey-Roasted Root Vegetables

Serves 6

1 sweet potato, scrubbed, coarsely chopped
1 medium turnip, peeled, coarsely chopped
1 medium parsnip, scrubbed, coarsely chopped
1 large carrot, scrubbed, coarsely chopped
1 tablespoon honey
1 teaspoon olive oil
½ cup shallots, halved
Cooking spray

Directions:

1. Preheat oven to 450°F.
2. Combine all ingredients except cooking spray in a large bowl; toss to coat.
3. Place vegetable mixture on a baking pan coated with cooking spray.
4. Bake for 30 minutes or until vegetables are tender and begin to brown, stirring every 15 minutes.

Nutrient Analysis: cal 72/pro 1/carb 16/fiber 2/fat 1/sodium 38

Exchanges: 1 bread

Adapted from Cooking Light Magazine, December 2007

Roasted Potatoes with Garlic and Rosemary

Serves 4

4 medium (about 1 pound) Yukon gold or red potatoes, unpeeled, cut into large chunks
½ tablespoon olive oil
2 cloves garlic, smashed
½ tablespoon fresh rosemary, chopped
¼ teaspoon ground black pepper

Directions:

1. Preheat oven to 450°F with rack in lower third.
2. Combine potato chunks with oil, garlic, and rosemary in a freezer zip top bag and empty onto a large baking sheet.
3. Roast potatoes in oven on lower rack for 20-30 minutes, or until fork tender, turning with spatula once during cooking.
4. Season with sea salt and black pepper as desired.

Nutrient Analysis: cal 100/pro 2/carb 19/fiber 2/fat 2/sodium 7

Exchanges: 1 bread

Adapted from Cuisine At Home Magazine

Stove-Top Home-Fried Potatoes

or Sweet Potatoes

Serves 1

1 medium white potato
OR
1 medium sweet potato
Cooking spray

Directions:

1. Scrub potato, prick with fork and microwave for 3 minutes or bake in 425 oven for 45 minutes.
2. Cut potato into quarters.
3. Heat skillet over medium and coat with cooking spray. Cook until golden brown on all sides, stirring often.
4. Season as desired.

Nutrient Analysis: cal 81/pro 2/carb 19/fiber 3/fat 0/sodium 27

Exchanges: 1 Bread

Vegetables

Vegetables add many nutrients, color, texture and volume to our meals. A must-have in our society where antioxidants and other disease-fighting chemicals are needed to maintain health. The colors in vegetables signify specific micro-nutrients, such as the red in peppers and tomatoes – lycopene is a potent cancer fighter. Purple, found in cabbage and many berries, contains anthocyanin, which promotes brain health. There are many wonderful ways to prepare vegetables for anyone's palate. Strive for half of the plate full of these powerhouse foods!

Braised Bok Choy

Serves 4

6 cups baby bok choy, cut lengthwise (or 3 regular, chunked)
1½ teaspoons Liquid Aminos or low-sodium soy sauce
1 cup shitake mushrooms, coarsely chopped
1 clove garlic, chopped
1½ teaspoons sesame seeds, lightly toasted

Directions:

1. Cover bottom of large skillet with ½ inch water. Add bok choy; drizzle with Liquid Aminos. Cover and cook on high heat until bok choy is tender, about 6 minutes.
2. Remove bok choy and add mushrooms and garlic to the liquid. Simmer liquid until reduced to a glaze and mushrooms are tender. Pour over bok choy and top with toasted sesame seeds.

Nutrient Analysis: cal 51/pro 3/carb 10/fiber 3/fat 1/sodium 85.5

Exchanges: 2 vegetable

Adapted from "Eat for Health" by Joel Fuhrman, M.D.

Garlicky Mustard Greens

Serves 4

1 pound mustard greens
1 teaspoon olive oil
½ cup onion, chopped
2 cloves garlic, minced
½ cup red bell pepper, chopped
¼ cup chicken broth, non-fat, lower-sodium
2 teaspoons cider vinegar
½ teaspoon sugar

Directions:

1. Wash greens well. Remove stems and any wilted leaves.
2. Stack several leaves, roll up and cut crosswise into 1-inch slices. Repeat with remaining greens.
3. Heat oil in Dutch oven or large saucepan over medium heat. Add onion and garlic; cook and stir 5 minutes until onion is tender.
4. Stir in greens, bell pepper and broth. Reduce heat to low. Cook, covered, 25 minutes or until greens are tender, stirring occasionally.
5. Combine vinegar and sugar in small cup; stir until sugar is dissolved. Stir into cooked greens; remove from heat and serve immediately.

Nutrient Analysis: cal 59/pro 4/carb 10/fiber 4/fat 2/sodium 38

Exchanges: 2 vegetable

Adapted from Diabetic Cooking

Broccoli Sunburst

Serves 6

2 - 10 ounce packages frozen broccoli spears or fresh broccoli
1 tablespoon butter, no added salt
1 tablespoon lemon juice
2 egg whites
2 tablespoons mayonnaise, reduced-fat
2 tablespoons parmesan cheese, grated
½ teaspoon paprika
2 tablespoons ground flax

Directions:

1. Cook broccoli according to directions.
2. Melt butter; stir in lemon juice and set aside.
3. Preheat broiler and place rack on middle to low shelf.
4. Beat egg whites until stiff. Gently fold in mayonnaise. Arrange broccoli in a 10-inch pie plate with stems in center.
5. Pour lemon butter over flower portion of broccoli. Spoon egg white mixture over stems in center.
6. Mix parmesan, paprika, and ground flax together and sprinkle on top. Broil 2 to 3 minutes.

Nutrient Analysis: cal 62/pro 4/carb 5/fiber 2/fat 3/sodium 200

Exchanges: 1, vegetable, ½ meat, ½ fat

Sweet and Sour Braised Cabbage

Serves 8

2 slices Applegate smoked bacon, chopped
1 cups (about 1 medium) onion, thinly, vertically sliced
1 1/2 cups (about 1 medium) granny smith apple, peeled, cored, chopped
5 cups red cabbage, thinly sliced
1/2 cup apple cider
½ teaspoon red wine vinegar
1 tablespoons sugar
1/4 teaspoon kosher salt
1 clove (whole) pepper
1 bay leaf

Directions:

1. Cook bacon in a Dutch oven over medium-high heat until crisp. Remove bacon from pan, reserving 1 tablespoon drippings in pan; set bacon aside.
2. Add onion to drippings in pan; sauté 3 minutes.
3. Add apple to pan; sauté 2 minutes.
4. Add cabbage to pan; sauté 2 minutes.
5. Add cider and remaining ingredients; bring to a boil. Cover, reduce heat, and simmer 1 hour and 15 minutes or until cabbage is tender, stirring occasionally.
6. Discard cloves and bay leaf; sprinkle with bacon.

Nutrient Analysis: cal 57/pro 1.5/carb 11.5/fiber 2/fat 1/sodium 132

Exchanges: 1/2 fruit, 1 vegetable

Make it a Meal: Roast meats or poultry

Ann Taylor Pittman, Cooking Light Magazine, December 2008

Eggplant Parmesan

Serves 6

2 eggplants
1 cup pasta sauce
½ cup shredded cheese, low-fat mozzarella
2 tablespoons bread crumbs
2 tablespoons grated parmesan cheese, reduced-fat
Cooking spray

Directions:

1. Preheat oven to 425° F. Coat cookie sheet and a casserole/baking dish with cooking spray.
2. Slice eggplant into thin slices and place on sprayed cookie sheet. Spray tops of eggplant with cooking spray. Bake until tender-crisp, about 15 minutes, turning to brown both sides.
3. Layer casserole/baking dish from bottom to top with pasta sauce, eggplant, ¼ cup shredded cheese, breadcrumbs, remaining shredded and parmesan cheeses.
4. Bake until sauce is bubbly and cheese is melted, about 20-25 minutes.

Nutrient Analysis: cal 100/pro 5/carb 16/fiber 7/fat 2/sodium 356

Exchanges: 1 meat, 2 vegetable

Crispy Zucchini Slices

Serves 4

2 small zucchini w/skin, scrubbed
1 medium egg
1 tablespoon water
⅓ cup bread crumbs
2 tablespoons parmesan cheese, reduced-fat, grated
Cooking spray

Directions:

1. Slice zucchini into thin slices.
2. In a bowl combine egg and water.
3. In a large plastic bag mix bread crumbs and parmesan cheese.
4. Dip zucchini slices in egg wash then shake in bag of breadcrumb mixture.
5. Heat large skillet over medium heat and coat with cooking spray.
6. Fry zucchini slices, turning at least once until both sides are crisp.

Nutrient Analysis: cal 51/pro 3/carb 5.5/fiber.5/fat 2/sodium 100

Exchanges: 1/2 meat, 1 vegetable

Appendix

Gluten Alternatives:
Gluten is found in wheat, rye, barley, spelt, kamut and some additives which are not used in this cookbook. The alternatives use here are flours, bread crumbs and crackers.

Instead of:	Try:
Flour	all-purpose gluten-free flour, rice, potato, buckwheat, fava bean or any noted gluten free flour
Bread crumbs	gluten free bread crumbs, usually made from rice
Cracker crumbs	crushed gluten free crackers, crushed gluten-free chips, oats (example-i may use oats if out of crackers for meatloaf)
Dairy alternatives:	
Milk	almond, rice, hemp, coconut, soy milk note: almond and rice milks are thinner, more like skim milk. Unsweetened soy, coconut and hemp milks have more body and thicken well in soups or in a roux
Sour cream or greek yogurt	plain coconut yogurt
Cream cheese	soy cream cheese

Cheese	vegan cheeses, daiya cheese-like shreds note: rice and almond cheeses have casein thus are not appropriate for true dairy allergy, but may work in dairy sensitive cases, as well as goat cheese, which has a similar protein structure to dairy but is slightly different
Condensed and evaporated Milks	unsweetened or plain coconut milk

Egg Substitutes:

There are many ingredients which can also be used as complete replacements for egg, if you are allergic to them. Thus, if you want to know some more egg substitute equivalents, read the following information.

1 egg = 2 Tbsp potato starch
1 egg = ¼ cup canned pumpkin or squash
1 egg = ¼ cup puréed prunes
1 egg = ¼ cup mashed potatoes
1 egg = 2 Tbsp water + 1 Tbsp oil + 2 tsp baking powder
1 egg = 1 Tbsp ground flax seed simmered in 3 Tbsp water
1 egg white = 1 Tbsp plain agar powder dissolved in 1 Tbsp water, whipped, chilled, and whipped again.

Lowering Fat In Recipes:

In dressings, use 1 part oil to 3 parts vinegar or lemon juice and 2 parts water. Use herbs and spices as desired. Two tablespoons equals 1 fat serving.

Use all temperature pan sprays for pre-greasing pans and to top crusted meat/fish/poultry recipes that require crisping or the browning reaction in the oven.

Cooking Grains:
Whole grains offer fiber, B-vitamins, some minerals, and are a delightful way to add bulk and fullness to a meal. Listed below are approximate cooking times and yield
for various grains.

1 Cup Uncooked/Water	Time/Yield
Pearl barley/3 cups	30-45 minutes/3 cups
Brown rice/2 cups (2 ½ for long grain)	45 minutes/3 cups
Buckwheat (kasha)/2 cups	15 minutes/2 ½ cups
Bulgur/2 cups	15-20 minutes/2 ½ cups
Cracked wheat/2 cups	25-30 minutes/2 ½ cups
Millet/3 cups	30-45 minutes/3 ½ cups
Rolled oats/2 ½ cups	10 minutes/3 cups
Triticale/3 cups	1 hour 15 minutes/3 ½ cups
Whole wheat berries/3 cups	2 hours/2 2/3 cups

Author Biography

Julie Freeman, MA, RD, LD, RYT

I am a licensed nutritionist with an education in nutrition science, home economics and psychology. My education in the home economics department required many hours of food preparation, experimental cooking and creating ambiance at the table. In this course of work, we were required to learn about creating recipes, following directions, planning the timing for preparation and cooking. As mentioned throughout my Introduction, I have been interested in cooking and healthy nutrition for many years, starting with baking as a child and followed by my own personal struggle with weight and compulsive eating. Following my years of study in college, I have continued to use my skills and develop my passion in healthy cooking in greater depth.

Since my teen years, I have been the hostess of parties and this has extended into my adult life with hosting parties for up to 100 people. I love the planning process from creating the menu, to planning the timetable for foods to be prepared ahead of time, and how this will all present on the table for taste and eye-appeal. I am usually the contact person for creating social occasions in my professional world as well.

I have been featured on both Channels Four and Seven highlighting nutrition topics. In the 80's, Look Magazine, Channel Four, had me prepare a meal and talk about the healthy aspects of tofu and vegetarian nutrition. The Channel Seven news filmed me on occasion – once at New England Memorial Hospital in Stoneham regarding childhood obesity, another time at the supermarket cruising the aisles and examining labels for heart healthy food choices.

I have written extensively for newspapers over the years and will attach one article published a year ago about the brain and food addiction. I am frequently asked to be a guest lecturer at schools, colleges and universities, and for private organizations, as well as to present seminars to a variety of audiences.

This book is to be the first in a series of books from **"Feel Great, Look Great ... from the inside out"**. Other books will address challenging our core negative beliefs in order to create a successful reality; wardrobing and colors that accentuate one's inner beauty to help with outward self-esteem; basic facial care and make-up that again accents our individual aspects of beauty while being safe from cancer and allergy causing chemicals. This series is a "cookbook" in and of itself – a total package for celebrating and accentuating the beauty of you!

I am passionate about my work and have an eager desire to reach many with enthusiasm and helpful tools for beginning to create a healthy lifestyle. I feel well-prepared to begin the journey of publishing and to take my message on the road!

IS YOUR BRAIN ADDICTED TO FOOD?
J FREEMAN, MA, RD, LD

Given the current statistics on obesity and addiction in general, there is rising research about the potential link between the foods we consume and food addiction. There appears to be differences in individuals' types of responses to environmental cues that influence the reward patterns in the brain. Focus has shifted to investigating the role that dopamine (a brain chemical messenger or neurotransmitter) plays in the reward system.

Many people persistently overeat despite considerable efforts to not do so! Experts are currently suggesting that our "obesogenic" food environment exposes people to high concentrations of addictive food substances - refined sweeteners, refined carbohydrates, fat, salt and caffeine, thus creating an environment in which they lose control over the ability to regulate intake. While there is no official definition for food addiction, some addiction researchers have defined it as:

Eating too much despite consequences, even those dire to health
Being preoccupied with food, food preparation and meals
Trying and failing to regulate food intake
Feeling guilty about eating and overeating

People with food addiction tend to display many of the same characteristics of those with other substance addictions - they tend to have common brain chemistries and similar experiences of mood altering effects from the consumption of certain foods. In fact the CAGE tool used for diagnosing alcoholism can be applied to food addiction:

Feeling the need to **Cut** down on the behavior
Feeling **Annoyed** with others' comments and criticisms
Feeling **Guilty** about eating
Feeling a need for the food first thing upon awakening - an **Eye-opener**

If this paints a dismal picture about the current food environment, what can be done to treat and prevent food addiction? The first thing to remember is that each person's brain responds differently and it is very important to recognize individual variability, as well as to look honestly at the potential for food addiction based on family history and personal history.

From a food perspective, try the following:
Increase protein* - 1 gram per kilo body weight
Increase fiber* - 3 grams or more per serving of grain food

Decrease sugar and all sweeteners, even sugar-free - 6 grams sugar
or less per serving Increase monounsaturated fats (olive and
canola oils, avocado and nuts) and omega three fats (fish,
flaxseed and walnuts)
Decrease saturated and trans fats**

*Grehlin is a gut hormone that increases appetite. Both protein and
fiber inhibit grehlin.
**Leptin is a gut hormone that decreases appetite. A high fat diet,
especially one high in saturated and trans fats, will inhibit
leptin.

What about Super Supplements?
Supplements are usually a second tier of treatment when it comes to
food addiction, but are nonetheless, very important in assisting in the
process of creating balance biochemically. A few of the top supplements to consider include:
Omega 3 fatty acids - assist in neurotransmitter communica-
tion and protection of the nerves in the brain
B complex vitamins - with folic acid ideally in the methyl
tetrahydrofolate form for the bioavailable form of folate. B
complex vitamins have a variety of functions including the
assistance of positive mood and release of energy from food
Amino Acids including dl-Phenylalanine, L-Tyrosine,
L-Glutamine* - assist with energy, mood and suppression of
cravings
5-HTP (Hydroxytryptophan)* - an amino acid that is the precursor to serotonin, the "feel good" neurotransmitter, also known
for appetite control
Chromium - a mineral that assists in glucose/insulin regulation.
Helps with maintaining stable energy and blood sugar
*Caution must be used for people on psychoactive medications. As
with any supplement, always discuss with your health care provider to
cross-reference supplements and medications for interactions.

While this may seem depressing to some, it actually is good news. Science is in a time of discovery about some of the reasons "why" people have such difficulty managing what should be simple - nourishment of our bodies with food. Food need not be the battle-field that it has become, but making changes toward a healthier diet is indeed a process - a process that need not be judged, but treated with compassion, understanding and a commitment to learn and listen to the language of the brain.

Julie Freeman, MA, RD, LD, is a nutritionist in private practice, who specializes in feeding issues of all types - food allergies, gastrointestinal disorders, eating disorders and disordered eating. Julie's approach to wellness combines the best of traditional and non-traditional nutrition therapy.

For more information, Julie can be reached at:
781-237-9016/juliefreeman57@gmail.com/www.juliefreeman.net

Made in the USA
Middletown, DE
18 December 2015